M000115349

DISPUTE RESOLUTION

1995 Supplement

EDITORIAL ADVISORY BOARD

Little, Brown and Company
Law and Business Education

Richard A. Epstein
James Parker Hall Distinguished Service Professor of Law
University of Chicago

E. Allan Farnsworth
Alfred McCormack Professor of Law
Columbia University

Ronald J. Gilson
Charles J. Meyers Professor of Law and Business
Stanford University
Marc and Eva Stern Professor of Law and Business
Columbia University

Geoffrey C. Hazard, Jr.
Trustee Professor of Law
University of Pennsylvania

James E. Krier
Earl Warren DeLano Professor of Law
University of Michigan

Elizabeth Warren
William A. Schnader Professor of Commercial Law
University of Pennsylvania

Bernard Wolfman
Fessenden Professor of Law
Harvard University

DISPUTE RESOLUTION

Negotiation, Mediation, and Other Processes

1995 Supplement

With Additional Exercises in Negotiation, Mediation, and Other Dispute Resolution Techniques

STEPHEN B. GOLDBERG

Professor of Law
Northwestern University

FRANK E.A. SANDER

Bussey Professor of Law
Harvard University

NANCY H. ROGERS

Professor of Law
Ohio State University

Little, Brown and Company
Boston   New York   Toronto   London

Copyright © 1995 by Stephen B. Goldberg, Frank E. A. Sander, and
Nancy H. Rogers

All rights reserved. No part of this book may be reproduced in any
form or by any electronic or mechanical means including
information storage and retrieval systems without permission in
writing from the publisher, except by a reviewer who may quote brief
passages in a review.

Library of Congress Catalog No. 92-70816
ISBN 0-316-31911-2

CCP
Published simultaneously in Canada
by Little, Brown & Company (Canada) Limited
Printed in the United States of America

Table of Contents

Table of Contents

Table of Cases

Preface

The purpose of this Supplement is twofold. Primarily, we seek to keep *Dispute Resolution* current by including references to important legal developments and to significant publications since the appearance of the second edition three years ago. In addition, we have developed a number of new simulations and other questions and problems that we believe teachers will find useful.

For each new exercise, as in the casebook, there is general information to be shared by all the participants. That information is contained in this Supplement. For most of the exercises, however, there is also confidential information for each side to consider, which is contained only in the Professor's Update to the Teacher's Manual to *Dispute Resolution* (available from Little, Brown). The Professor's Update contains instructions on the use of the confidential information, and Teaching Notes.

The Supplement follows the same format used in the casebook. Footnotes and other references (such as citations in judicial opinions) are generally omitted from the excerpts; footnotes that have not been omitted retain their original numbering. Our own footnotes are indicated by asterisks.

S.B.G.
F.E.A.S.
N.H.R.

April 1995

Acknowledgments

The authors gratefully acknowledge the permissions granted to reproduce excerpts from the following materials.

BRETT, Jeanne M., Stephen B. GOLDBERG, and William L. URY (1994) "Managing Conflict: The Strategy of Dispute Systems Design," 6 *Bus. Wk. Executive Briefing Service*. Adapted with permission of McGraw-Hill, Inc.

BUSH, Robert A. Baruch and Joseph P. FOLGER (1994) *The Promise of Mediation*. San Francisco: Jossey-Bass. Reprinted by permission.

LEWIS, Michael (forthcoming) "Advocacy in Mediation: One Mediator's View," *Disp. Resol. Mag.* (Fall 1995). Reprinted by permission.

MCEWEN, Craig A., and Nancy ROGERS (1994) "Bring the Lawyers into Divorce Mediation," *Disp. Resol. Mag.* 8 (Summer). Reprinted by permission.

MNOOKIN, Robert H. (1993) "Why Negotiations Fail: An Exploration of Barriers to the Resolution of Conflict," 8 *Ohio St. J. on Disp. Resol.* 235. Reprinted by permission.

MNOOKIN, Robert H., and Ronald J. GILSON (1994) "Cooperation and Conflict Between Litigators," 12 *Alternatives* 125. Copyright © by the CPR Institute for Dispute Resolution. Reprinted by permission.

PEARSON, Jessica (1994) "Family Mediation," in *National Symposium on Court-Connected Dispute Resolution Research: A Report on Current Research Findings* 51. Alexandria, VA: State Justice Institute. Reprinted by permission.

SANDER, Frank E.A., and Stephen B. GOLDBERG (1994) "Fitting the Forum to the Fuss: A User-Friendly Guide to Selecting an ADR Procedure," 10 *Negotiation J.* 49. Reprinted by permission.

SHELL, G. Richard (1991) "When Is It Legal to Lie in Negotiations?" *Sloan Mgmt. Rev. 93* (Spring). Reprinted by permission of publisher. Copyright © 1991 by the Sloan Management Review Association. All rights reserved.

SHERMAN, Edward (1993) "Court-Mandated Alternative Dispute Resolution: What Form of Participation Should Be Required?" 46 *SMU L. Rev.* 2079. Reprinted by permission.

SIEDEL, George J. (1986) "The Decision Tree: A Method to Figure Litigation Risks," *B. Leader* 18 (Jan.-Feb.). Reprinted by permission.

The authors acknowledge further the permissions granted to reproduce the following exercises.

Caroline's Donut Shop. Reprinted by permission of Cheryl B. McDonald, Pepperdine University School of Law, and Nancy Rogers, Ohio State University Law School.

Nam Choi v. Austin University Medical School. Reprinted by permission of Thomas O. Patrick, Lecturer in Law, College of Law, West Virginia University.

Prosando v. High-Tech. Copyright © 1994 by the CPR Institute for Dispute Resolution. Reprinted by permission.

Southern Electric Company and Public Utility Workers Union, AFL-CIO. Reprinted by permission of Mediation Research & Education Project, Inc., Northwestern University Law School, Chicago, Illinois.

DISPUTE RESOLUTION

1995 Supplement

Chapter 1
Disputing Procedures

Page 12. Add to the References:

DAUER, Edward A. (1994) *Manual of Dispute Resolution.* Colorado Springs: Shepards-McGraw Hill.

Chapter 2

Negotiation

Page 73.   Add the following article before the Questions:

R. MNOOKIN AND R. GILSON, COOPERATION AND CONFLICT BETWEEN LITIGATORS*

12 Alternatives 125 (CPR Institute for Dispute Resolution 1994)

Do lawyers facilitate dispute resolution or do they instead exacerbate conflict and pose a barrier to the efficient resolution of disputes? Today, the popular view is that lawyers magnify the inherent divisiveness of dispute resolution. According to this vision, . . . litigators rarely cooperate to resolve disputes efficiently. Instead, shielded by a professional ideology that is said to require zealous advocacy, they wastefully fight in ways that enrich themselves but rarely advantage their clients.

But purveyor of needless conflict need not be the only vision of the lawyer's role in litigation. More than a century ago, Abraham Lincoln suggested that as peacemakers lawyers might facilitate efficient and fair resolution of conflict when their clients could not do it for themselves. In an article we recently published in the *Columbia Law Review* we offered a conceptual foundation for this perspective. It rests on the idea that lawyers may allow clients to cooperate in circumstances when the clients could not do so on their own. . . .

The central idea should be familiar to most practicing lawyers: a trusting relationship between two opposing lawyers permits them to rely confidently on each other's representations and can substantially improve the efficiency of the dispute resolution process. When opposing

*Copyright © 1994 by CPR Institute for Dispute Resolution, 366 Madison Avenue, New York, NY 10017. Reprinted with permission. The CPR Institute for Dispute Resolution is a nonprofit initiative of 500 general counsel of major corporations, leading law firms, and prominent legal academics in support of private alternatives to the high costs of litigation. Organized in 1979 as the Center for Public Resources/CPR Legal Program, CPR develops new methods to resolve business and public disputes by alternative dispute resolution (ADR).

lawyers value their reputations with each other for trustworthiness and cooperation, they can create an environment for collaborative problem solving even in circumstances where their clients cannot.

LITIGATION AS A PRISONER'S DILEMMA: WHY COOPERATION IS DIFFICULT

. . . In many disputes, each litigant may want to cooperate but may instead feel compelled to make a contentious move to avoid exploitation by the other side. No one wants to be a "sucker" by cooperating and be taken advantage of by someone who won't cooperate. This combination of contentious moves that neither really wanted to take, results in a less efficient outcome than if the litigants had been able to cooperate.

Consider a highly simplified example. Suppose two disputants have a choice: each must independently decide whether to cooperate by voluntarily disclosing all material information to the other side (including some that is unfavorable) or to defect by withholding information, thereby forcing the other side to engage in expensive discovery to dig out some but not all of the unfavorable information.

The payoff structure in these circumstances may resemble that of the classical prisoner's dilemma. The worse payoff—the "sucker's payoff"—goes to a player who cooperates while the other player defects. The best payoff goes to a defector whose opponent has cooperated. The other two possible outcomes—mutual cooperation and mutual defection—fall somewhere between these two extremes, with the reward for mutual cooperation being better than the payoff for mutual defection.

Clients may prefer mutual cooperation to mutual defection but be unwilling to cooperate for fear of getting the sucker's payoff, especially if the clients do not expect to have future dealings with each other. If the disputants do not trust each other to resist the temptation to defect, they may lack the credibility to be viewed as bound by their own good intentions. The net result is that both may defect and thus end up with a worse payoff than if both had cooperated.

HOW LAWYERS CAN HELP

Lawyers, unlike many disputants, are repeat players who have the opportunity to establish reputations for cooperation—reputations that would be lost if they defected. Our central point is that disputing parties can avoid the prisoner's dilemma inherent in much litigation by selecting cooperative lawyers whose reputations credibly commit each party to a cooperative strategy.

To illustrate, imagine a "pre-litigation game" in which clients disclose their choice of lawyer beforehand. Then imagine a world in which lawyers are clearly divided into two groups: gladiators and cooperative lawyers. Under the assumptions of our pre-litigation game, disputing through lawyers provides an escape from the prisoner's dilemma. If one client chooses a cooperative lawyer and her opponent chooses a gladiator, the client choosing a cooperative lawyer can change her lawyer without cost before the game starts. She has made a commitment, but it is conditional on what the other side does.

With this assumption, each client's dominant strategy is to choose a cooperative lawyer, because the choice of a cooperative lawyer binds each client to a cooperative strategy. If client A chooses a cooperative lawyer and client B also chooses a cooperative lawyer, both clients receive the cooperative payoff.

This suggests that there might be a market for cooperative lawyers. Both parties to a lawsuit with a prisoner's dilemma payoff structure would like to hire cooperative lawyers, because that allows them to commit to a cooperative strategy. Clients should therefore be willing to pay cooperative lawyers a premium, reflecting a portion of the amount by which the cooperative payoff exceeds the noncooperative payoff. Cooperative lawyers would not later defect, even at their clients' urging, because that would cost them their valuable reputations.

Of course the real world of litigation is much more complicated than the abstract models of game theory. Not all litigation has a payoff structure like that of a prisoner's dilemma. And in litigation it often may be difficult to assess whether the other side is in fact cooperating or not. Nevertheless, we believe the prisoner's dilemma provides a powerful metaphor for understanding the barriers to cooperative behavior inherent in many legal disputes. Indeed, we found that our analysis helped us understand more fully why there appears to be more cooperating in some practice settings than in others.

COMMERCIAL LITIGATION

The general public holds the view that in recent years the conduct of commercial litigation has deteriorated, and cooperation has diminished. The amount of commercial litigation has increased dramatically. A concomitant increase in uncivil conduct has been marked most noticeably by discovery abuse.

The prisoner's dilemma heuristic suggests a reason: Some commercial litigation has payoffs in which one party does not gain from mutual cooperation. In that case the dominant strategy for both parties is conflict, not cooperation. For example, as the spread between the statutory and market interest rates increases as it did in the 1970s, it becomes more likely that the defendant's dominant strategy will be noncooperation. The gains from the spread as a result of delay outweigh the transaction costs of the conflict. . . .

[T]he 1980s . . . brought an increase in strategic litigation—using litigation to gain a business advantage by imposing costs on the opposing party. Trade secret cases against startup companies and suits against the bidder in hostile takeovers are examples. In strategic litigation, the dominant strategy for one party is noncooperation, and the other party responds in kind. . . .

Moreover, large case commercial litigation is quite "noisy." Clearly identifying whether the other side has cooperated or defected in a competitive environment where cooperation is defined as being not *too* conflictual, is often difficult. For a reputation market to work, defections by cooperative lawyers must be observable.

FAMILY LAW

In contrast to commercial litigation, family law practice shows persistent pockets of cooperation between opposing counsel. When we interviewed elite family lawyers in Northern California who are members of the American Academy of Matrimonial Lawyers, we found a surprising amount of cooperation. Lawyers knew who were the gladiators and who were the cooperative lawyers. With the exception of cases involving known gladiators, these lawyers routinely exchanged information and documents informally. Because opposing counsel knew and trusted each other, they rarely insisted on interrogatories or depositions or engaged in protracted formal discovery.

In applying the heuristic of the prisoner's dilemma to family law, it is obvious that the payoff structure must contain gains for cooperation and the risk of loss if the other party defects. Put in context, divorce litigation must be seen as more than a distributive (zero-sum) game in which the couple's property and children are divided.

Sometimes divorcing parents can devise arrangements that benefit both themselves and their children, but a number of potential barriers to cooperation make the divorce lawyer's role critical. When inexperience, inability or a soured relationship prevent divorcing spouses from cooperating, the cooperating divorce lawyers may provide an escape: by credibly committing their clients to cooperate, the lawyers as intermediaries may be able to create gains that the spouses could not realize alone.

6

The institutional structure of family law practice, which tends to be both localized and specialized, allows lawyers to create and sustain reputations as either cooperative problem-solvers or as more adversarial gladiators. Clients tend to seek lawyers with a particular orientation.

INSTITUTIONAL FEATURES THAT CAN MAKE A DIFFERENCE

What institutional features make cooperation more or less likely?

The comparison of commercial litigation and family law suggests that the following institutional features can influence how easily lawyers can facilitate cooperation between their clients: the size of the legal community, the incentives in the lawyers' practice setting, and the complexity of the legal environment.

- The larger the size of the legal community, the longer it will take to develop a reputation and to acquire sufficient information about the reputation of other lawyers. The size of the legal community also has a direct effect on lawyer conduct. When lawyers know each other, we can expect less tactical jockeying, harassment, evasion and other forms of resistance to disclosure.
- The organization of practice can influence the level of cooperation within the legal community, and that influence can run in either direction. Are lawyers paid by the hour or by outcome? In firms, on what basis are partnership profits divided—seniority or productivity? On what basis are associates promoted? Economic incentives for individual lawyers can influence the level of cooperation.
- Working against cooperation is the increasing complexity of litigation. As it increases, so do the opportunities for misunderstandings and unnecessary conflict. The more complicated the litigation, the more likely that innocent behavior may mistakenly be seen as defection, resulting in a pattern of responsive defections. From this perspective, the pre-litigation game takes on special significance. Not only does a party's choice of lawyer signal whether a party wishes to cooperate; it also signals the lawyer's evaluation of the lawsuit. A cooperative lawyer will not resort to being drawn into strategic litigation. . . .

HOW CAN COOPERATION BE FACILITATED?

Some institutional reforms could reduce the barriers to lawyers facilitating cooperation between their clients.

7

- "Zealous advocacy" for a lawyer is traditionally client-centered. For the lawyer seeking to establish or maintain a reputation for cooperation, this can pose a dilemma: what if a client asks the lawyer to defect? A clear statement that the Model Rules allows a client to "tie its hands" at the time of the lawyer's engagement—to give the cooperative lawyer the right to withdraw rather than defect later in the litigation—would remove that barrier. This works to the benefit of a cooperative client: Only then could a client credibly commit to cooperation, and only then could a lawyer be able to protect his or her investment in a reputation for cooperation. . . .
- Another way to facilitate cooperation might be to develop a professional organization that limited its membership to lawyers who specialized in cooperative representation. Such an organization could enhance the reputation of its members and serve as a powerful "stamp of approval.". . .

A professional organization would help to clarify norms within specific practice areas. Unlike the world of the prisoner's dilemma, where the meaning of each move is clear, the real world is noisy and ambiguous. One useful role for a professional organization would be to clarify what cooperation or defection means in the context of particular kinds of disputes and to describe how lawyers might cooperate in a given context. A professional group also could develop requirements of cooperative representation, promulgate standards of conduct, and impose sanctions for non-compliance.

In short, the relationship between opposing lawyers and their capacity to establish credible reputations for cooperation have profound implications for dispute resolution. Lawyers develop reputations, and the reputation for being a cooperative problem-solver may be a valuable asset. When opposing lawyers know and trust each other, both parties often will benefit.

Page 73.   Add Question 2.5(a) to the Questions:

2.5(a) Suppose that two "cooperative" lawyers are engaged in a voluntary information exchange rather than formal adversarial discovery, with the implicit understanding that material information will not be withheld. One client then instructs his lawyer to withhold an important document. What can the lawyer do within the limits of the rules of professional conduct to protect her reputation as a cooperative lawyer? Could the lawyer deal with the problem by hinting to opposing counsel that she could no longer follow a cooperative strategy?

*Page 83.   Add the following introductory text and article
            before the Questions:*

A lawyer must be concerned not only with the ethical implications
of what she says—or does not say—in negotiations, but with the legal
implications as well. The latter topic is treated by Professor Shell in the
following article.

G. SHELL, WHEN IS IT LEGAL TO LIE IN NEGOTIATIONS?

Sloan Mgmt. Rev. 93, 94-96 (Spring 1991)

The elements of common law fraud are deceptively simple. A statement is fraudulent when the speaker makes a knowing misrepresentation of a material fact on which the victim reasonably relies and which
causes damages. . . .

KNOWING

The common law definition of fraud requires that the speaker have a
particular state of mind with respect to the fact he misrepresents: the
statement must be made "knowingly." This generally means that the
speaker knows what he says is false. One way of getting around fraud,
therefore, might be for the speaker to avoid contact with information
that would lead to a "knowing" state of mind. For example, a company
president might suspect that his company is in poor financial health, but
he does not yet "know" it because he has not seen the latest quarterly
reports. When his advisers ask to set up a meeting to discuss these reports,
he tells them to hold off. He is about to go into negotiations with an
important supplier and would like to be able to say, honestly, that so far
as he knows the company is paying its bills. Does this get the president off
the hook? No. The courts have stretched the definition of "knowing" to
include statements that are "reckless," that is, those made with a con-
scious disregard for their truth. Thus, when the information that will give
the speaker the truth is close at hand and he deliberately turns away in
order to maintain a convenient state of ignorance, the law will treat him
as if he spoke with full knowledge that his statements were false. . . .

MISREPRESENTATION

In general, the law requires the speaker to make a positive misstate-
ment before it will attach liability for fraud. Thus, a basic rule for

commercial negotiators is to "be silent and be safe." As a practical matter, of course, silence is difficult to maintain if one's bargaining opponent is an astute questioner. In the face of inconvenient questions, negotiators are often forced to resort to verbal feints and dodges such as, "I don't know about that," or, when pressed, "That is not a subject I am at liberty to discuss."

There are circumstances when such dodges will not do, and it may be fraudulent to keep your peace about an issue. When does a negotiator have a duty to frankly disclose matters that may hurt his bargaining position? Under recent cases, the law imposes affirmative disclosure duties in the following four circumstances:

1. *When the nondisclosing party makes a partial disclosure that is or becomes misleading in light of all the facts.* If you say your company is profitable, you may have a duty to disclose whether you used questionable accounting techniques to arrive at that statement. If you show a loss in the next quarter and negotiations are still ongoing, you may be required to disclose the loss. One way to avoid this is to make no statements on delicate subjects in the first place. Then you have no duty to correct or update yourself.

2. *When the parties stand in a fiduciary relationship to one another.* In negotiations involving trustees and beneficiaries, parties must be completely frank and cannot rely on the "be silent and be safe" rubric. Note, however, that courts have recently broadened the notion of a "fiduciary" to include banks, franchisors, and other commercial players who deal with business partners on a somewhat-less-than-arm's-length basis. In short, it is becoming increasingly risky to withhold important information in negotiations with parties who depend on you for their commercial well-being.

3. *When the nondisclosing party has "superior information" vital to the transaction that is not accessible to the other side.* This is a slippery exception, but the best test is one of conscience. Indeed, courts often state that the legal test of disclosure is whether "equity or good conscience" requires that the fact be revealed. Would you feel cheated if the other side didn't tell you about the hidden fact? Or would you secretly kick yourself for not having found it out yourself? If the former, you should consult an attorney. A recent case applying this exception held that an employer owed a duty to a prospective employee to disclose contingency plans for shutting down the project for which the employee was hired. In general, sellers have a greater duty than buyers to disclose things they know about their own property. Thus, a home seller must disclose termite infestation in her home. But an oil company need not disclose the existence of oil on a farmer's land when negotiating a purchase.

4. *When special transactions are at issue, such as insurance contracts.* Insur-

ers must fully disclose the scope of coverage, and insureds must fully disclose their insurance risk. If you apply for a life insurance policy and do not disclose your heart condition, you have committed fraud.

If none of these four exceptions applies, you are not likely to be found liable for common law fraud based on a nondisclosure. Beware of special statutory modifications of the common law rules, however. For example, if the sale of your company involves a purchase or sale of securities, state and federal antifraud rules may impose a stiffer duty of disclosure than may apply under the common law. . . .

MATERIAL

Most people lie about something during negotiations. Often they seek to deceive others by making initial demands that far exceed their true needs or desires. Sometimes they mislead others about their reservation price or "bottom line." Of course, demands and reservation prices may not be "facts." One may have only a vague idea of what one really wants or is willing to pay for something. Hence, a statement that an asking price is too high may not be a true misrepresentation as much as a statement of preference. Suppose, however, that a negotiator has been given authority by a seller to peddle an item for any price greater than $10,000. Is it fraud for the negotiator to reject an offer of $12,000 and state that the deal cannot be closed at that price? In fact, the deal could be closed for that price so there has been a knowing misrepresentation of fact. The question is whether this fact is material in a legal sense. It is not. . . .

Demands and reservation prices are not, as a matter of law, material to a deal. . . .

Some experienced negotiators may be surprised to learn, however, that there are legal problems when negotiators try to embellish their refusals to accept a particular price with supporting lies. Lies about "other offers" are classic problem cases of this sort. For example, take the following relatively older but still leading case from Massachusetts. A commercial landlord bought a building and proceeded to negotiate a new lease with a toy shop tenant when the tenant's lease expired. The proprietor of the toy shop bargained hard and refused to pay the landlord's demand for a $10,000 increase in rent. The landlord then told the shop owner that he had another tenant willing to pay the amount and threatened the current tenant with immediate eviction if he did not promptly agree to the new rate. The tenant paid, but learned several years later that the threat had been a bluff; there was no other tenant. The tenant sued successfully for fraud.

In a more recent case, this time from Oklahoma, a real estate agent was held liable for fraud, including *punitive* damages, when she pressured a buyer into closing on a home with a story that a rival buyer (the contractor who built the house) was willing to pay the asking price and would do so later that same day. In these cases, the made-up offer was a lie; it concerned an objective fact (either someone had made an offer or they had not), and the courts ruled that the lie could be material given all the circumstances.

Page 85.   Add Questions 2.18, 2.19, 2.20, and the following article after Question 2.17:

2.18   You are the attorney for the company president whom Shell describes as having "deliberately turn[ed] away in order to maintain a convenient state of ignorance" about the financial health of his company. The company president tells you about this just before the two of you enter negotiations with the "important supplier." Are you required by Rule 4.1 to disclose the president's fraud to the supplier?

2.19   Would it be fraudulent for the writer in Question 2.15 to fail to disclose the forthcoming taking of possession and bugle calls by the Blue Berets? If so, and the writer learned of the Blue Berets' purchase from you, his attorney, would you violate Rule 4.1 by nondisclosure?

2.20   In the example given by Shell in which the seller authorized his agent to accept any price over $10,000, suppose that the buyer's agent had asked her, "Are you authorized to accept $11,000?" Would it be fraudulent for the seller's agent to say "No"? If so, how should she respond to that question?

R. MNOOKIN, WHY NEGOTIATIONS FAIL: AN EXPLORATION OF BARRIERS TO THE RESOLUTION OF CONFLICT

8 Ohio St. J. on Disp. Resol. 235, 238-246, 248-249 (1993)

Conflict is inevitable, but efficient and fair resolution is not. Conflicts can persist even though there may be any number of possible resolutions that would better serve the interests of the parties. . . . In our everyday personal and professional lives, we have all witnessed disputes where the absence of a resolution imposes substantial and avoidable costs on all parties. Moreover, many resolutions that are achieved—whether through negotiation or imposition—conspicuously fail to satisfy the economist's criterion of Pareto efficiency. . . .

Why is it that under circumstances where there are resolutions that better serve disputants, negotiations often fail to achieve efficient resolutions? In other words, what are the barriers to the negotiated resolution of conflict?

A. STRATEGIC BARRIERS

The first barrier to the negotiated resolution of conflict is inherent in a central characteristic of negotiation. Negotiation can be metaphorically compared to making a pie and then dividing it up. The process of conflict resolution affects both the size of the pie, and who gets what size slice.

The disputants' behavior may affect the size of the pie in a variety of ways. On the one hand, spending on avoidable legal fees and other process costs shrinks the pie. On the other hand, negotiators can together "create value" and make the pie bigger by discovering resolutions in which each party contributes special complementary skills that can be combined in a synergistic way, or by exploiting differences in relative preferences that permit trades that make both parties better off. . . .

Negotiation also involves issues concerning the distribution of benefits, and, with respect to pure distribution, both parties cannot be made better off at the same time. Given a pie of fixed size, a larger slice for you means a smaller one for me.

Because bargaining typically entails both efficiency issues (that is, how big the pie can be made) and distributive issues (that is, who gets what size slice), negotiation involves an inherent tension—one that David Lax and James Sebenius have dubbed the "negotiator's dilemma." In order to create value, it is critically important that options be created in light of both parties' underlying interests and preferences. This suggests the importance of openness and disclosure, so that a variety of options can be analyzed and compared from the perspective of all concerned. However, when it comes to the distributive aspects of bargaining, full disclosure—particularly if unreciprocated by the other side—can often lead to outcomes in which the more open party receives a comparatively smaller slice. To put it another way, unreciprocated approaches to creating value leave their maker vulnerable to claiming tactics. On the other hand, focusing on the distributive aspects of bargaining can often lead to unnecessary deadlocks and, more fundamentally, a failure to discover options or alternatives that make both sides better off. . . .

Even when both parties know all the relevant information, and that potential gains may result from a negotiated deal, strategic bargaining over how to divide the pie can still lead to deadlock (with no deal at all) or protracted and expensive bargaining, thus shrinking the pie. For example, suppose Nancy has a house for sale for which she has a reservation price of $245,000. I am willing to pay up to $295,000 for the house. Any deal within a bargaining range from $245,000 to $295,000 would make both of us better off than no sale at all. Suppose we each know the other's reservation price. Will there be a deal? Not necessarily. If we disagree about how the $50,000 "surplus" should be divided (each wanting all or most of it), our negotiation may end in a deadlock. We might engage in hardball negotiation tactics in which each tried to persuade the other that he or she was committed to walking away from a beneficial deal, rather than accept less than $40,000 of the surplus. Nancy might claim that she won't take a nickel less than $285,000, or even $294,999 for that matter. Indeed, she might go so far as to give a power of attorney to an agent to sell only at that price, and then leave town in order to make her commitment credible. Of course, I could play the same type of game and the result would then be that no deal is made and that we are both worse off. In this case, the obvious tension between the distribution of the $50,000 and the value creating possibilities inherent in any sale within the bargaining range may result in no deal.

Strategic behavior—which may be rational for a self-interested party concerned with maximizing the size of his or her own slice—can often lead to inefficient outcomes. Those subjected to claiming tactics often respond in kind, and the net result typically is to push up the cost of the dispute resolution process. . . . Parties may be tempted to engage in strategic behavior, hoping to get more. Often all they do is shrink the size of the pie. Those experienced in the civil litigation process see this all the time. One or both sides often attempt to use pre-trial discovery as leverage to force the other side into agreeing to a more favorable settlement. Often the net result, however, is simply that both sides spend unnecessary money on the dispute resolution process.

B. THE PRINCIPAL/AGENT PROBLEM

The second barrier is suggested by recent work relating to transaction cost economics, and is sometimes called the "principal/agent" problem. . . . The basic problem is that the incentives for an agent (whether it be a lawyer, employee, or officer) negotiating on behalf of a party to a dispute may induce behavior that fails to serve the interests of the principal itself. The relevant research suggests that it is no simple matter—whether by contract or custom—to align perfectly the incentives for an agent with the interests of the principal. This divergence may act as a barrier to efficient resolution of conflict.

Litigation is fraught with principal/agent problems. In civil litigation, for example—particularly where the lawyers on both sides are being paid by the hour—there is very little incentive for the opposing lawyers to cooperate, particularly if the clients have the capacity to pay for trench warfare and are angry to boot. Commentators have suggested that this is one reason many cases settle on the courthouse steps, and not before: for the lawyers, a late settlement may avoid the possible embarrassment of an extreme outcome, while at the same time providing substantial fees. . . .

C.   COGNITIVE BARRIERS

The third barrier is a by-product of the way the human mind processes information, deals with risks and uncertainties, and makes inferences and judgments. Research by cognitive psychologists during the last fifteen years suggests several ways in which human reasoning often departs from that suggested by theories of rational judgment and decision making. . . .

Suppose everyone attending this evening's lecture is offered the following happy choice: At the end of my lecture you can exit at the north end of the hall or the south end. If you choose the north exit, you will be handed an envelope in which there will be a crisp new twenty dollar bill. Instead, if you choose the south exit, you will be given a sealed envelope randomly pulled from a bin. One quarter of these envelopes contain a $100 bill, but three quarters are empty. In other words, you can have a sure gain of $20 if you go out the north door, or you can instead gamble by choosing the south door where you will have a 25% chance of winning $100 and a 75% chance of winning nothing. Which would you choose? A great deal of experimental work suggests that the overwhelming majority of you would choose the sure gain of $20, even though the "expected value" of the second alternative, $25, is slightly more. This is a well known phenomenon called "risk aversion." The principle is that most people will take a sure thing over a gamble, even where the gamble may have a somewhat higher "expected" payoff.

Daniel Kahneman and Amos Tversky have advanced our understanding of behavior under uncertainty with a remarkable discovery. They suggest that, in order to avoid what would otherwise be a sure loss, many people will gamble, even if the expected loss from the gamble is larger. Their basic idea can be illustrated by changing my hypothetical. Although you didn't know this when you were invited to this lecture, it is not free. At the end of the lecture, the doors are going to be locked. If you go out the north door, you'll be required to *pay* $20 as an exit fee. If you go out the south door, you'll participate in a lottery by drawing an envelope. Three quarters of the time you're going to be let out for free, but one quarter of the time you're going to be required to pay $100. Rest assured all the money is going to the Dean's fund—a very good cause. What do you choose? There's a great deal of empirical research, based on the initial work of Kahneman and Tversky, suggesting that the majority of this audience would choose the south exit—i.e., most of you would gamble to avoid having to lose $20 for sure. Kahneman and Tversky call this "loss aversion."

Now think of these two examples together. Risk aversion suggests that most of you would not gamble for a gain, even though the expected value of $25 exceeds the sure thing of $20. On the other hand, most of you would gamble to avoid a sure loss, even though, on the average, the loss of going out the south door is higher. Experimental evidence suggests that the proportion of people who will gamble to avoid a loss is much greater than those who would gamble to realize a gain.

Loss aversion can act as a cognitive barrier to the negotiated resolution of conflict for a variety of reasons. For example, both sides may fight on in a dispute in the hope that they may avoid any losses, even though the continuation of the dispute involves a gamble in which the loss may end up being far greater. Loss aversion may explain Lyndon Johnson's decision, in 1965, to commit additional troops to Vietnam as an attempt to avoid the sure loss attendant to withdrawal, and as a gamble that there might be some way in the future to avoid any loss at all. Similarly, negotiators may, in some circumstances, be adverse to offering a concession in circumstances where they view the concession as a sure loss. Indeed, the notion of rights or entitlements may be associated with a more extreme form of loss aversion that Kahneman and Tversky call "enhanced loss aversion," because losses "compounded by outrage are much less acceptable than losses that are caused by misfortune or by legitimate actions of others."

One of the most striking features of loss aversion is that whether something is viewed as a gain or loss—and what kind of gain or loss it is considered—depends upon a reference point, and the choice of a reference point is sometimes manipulable. Once again, a simple example suggested by Kahneman and Tversky, can illustrate.

Suppose you and a friend decide to go to Cleveland for a big night out on the town. You've made reservations at an elegant restaurant that will cost $100 a couple. In addition, you've bought two superb seats—at $50 each—to hear the Cleveland orchestra. You set off for Cleveland, thinking you have your symphony tickets and $100, but no credit cards.

Imagine that you park your car in Cleveland and make a horrifying discovery—you've lost the tickets. Assume that you cannot be admitted to the symphony without tickets. Also imagine that someone is standing in front of the Symphony Hall offering to sell two tickets for $100. You have a choice. You can use the $100 you intended for the fancy dinner to buy the tickets to hear the concert, or you can skip the concert and simply go to dinner. What would you do?

Consider a second hypothetical. After you park your car, you look in your wallet and you realize to your horror that the $100 is gone, but the tickets are there. In front of the Symphony Hall is a person holding a small sign indicating she would like to buy two tickets for $100. What do you do? Do you sell the tickets and go to dinner? Or do you instead skip dinner and simply go to the concert?

Experimental research suggests that in the first example many more people will skip the symphony and simply go out to dinner, while in the second example, the proportions are nearly reversed; most people would skip dinner and go to the concert. The way we keep our mental accounts is such that, in the first instance, to buy the tickets a second time would somehow be to overspend our ticket budget. And, yet, an economist would point out that the two situations are essentially identical because there is a ready and efficient market in which you can convert tickets to money or money to tickets.

The purpose of the hypotheticals is to suggest that whether or not an event is framed as a loss can often affect behavior. This powerful idea concerning "framing" has important implications for the resolution of disputes to which I will return later.

D.   "REACTIVE DEVALUATION" OF COMPROMISES AND CONCESSIONS

The final barrier I wish to discuss is "reactive devaluation," and is an example of a social/psychological barrier that arises from the dynamics of the negotiation process and the inferences that negotiators draw from their interactions. My Stanford colleague, psychology Professor Lee Ross, and his students have done experimental work to suggest that, especially between adversaries, when one side offers a particular concession or proposes a particular exchange of compromises, the other side may diminish the attractiveness of that offer or proposed exchange simply because it originated with a perceived opponent. The basic notion is a familiar one, especially for lawyers. How often have you had a client indicate to you in the midst of litigation, "If only we could settle this case for $7,000. I'd love to put this whole matter behind me." Lo and behold, the next day, the other side's attorney calls and offers to settle for $7,000. You excitedly call your client and say, "Guess what—the other side has just offered to settle this case for $7,000." You expect to hear jubilation on the other end of the phone, but instead there is silence. Finally, your client says, "Obviously they must know something we don't know. If $7,000 is a good settlement for them, it can't be a good settlement for us."

Both in laboratory and field settings, Ross and his colleagues have marshalled interesting evidence for "reactive devaluation." They have demonstrated both that a given compromise proposal is rated less positively when proposed by someone on the other side than when proposed by a neutral or an ally. They also demonstrated that a concession that is actually offered is rated lower than a concession that is withheld, and that a compromise is rated less highly after it has been put on the table by the other side than it was beforehand. . . .

III.   OVERCOMING STRATEGIC BARRIERS: THE ROLES OF NEGOTIATORS AND MEDIATORS

The study of barriers can do more than simply help us understand why negotiations sometimes fail when they should not. It can also contribute to our understanding of how to overcome these barriers. Let me illustrate this by using the preceding analysis of four barriers briefly to explore the role of mediators, and to suggest why neutrals can often facilitate the efficient resolution of disputes by overcoming these specific barriers.

First, let us consider the strategic barrier. To the extent that a neutral third party is trusted by both sides, the neutral may be able to induce the parties to reveal information about their underlying interests, needs, priorities, and aspirations that they would not disclose to their adversary. This information may permit a trusted mediator to help the parties enlarge the pie in circumstances where the parties acting alone could not. Moreover, a mediator can foster a problem-solving atmosphere and lessen the temptation on the part of each side to engage in strategic behavior. A skilled mediator can often get parties to move beyond political posturing and recriminations about past wrongs and to instead consider possible gains from a fair resolution of the dispute.

A mediator also can help overcome barriers posed by principal/ agent problems. A mediator may bring clients themselves to the table, and help them understand their shared interest in minimizing legal fees and costs in circumstances where the lawyers themselves might not be doing so. In circumstances where a middle manager is acting to prevent a settlement that might benefit the company, but might be harmful to the manager's own career, an astute mediator can sometimes bring another company representative to the table who does not have a personal stake in the outcome.

A mediator can also promote dispute resolution by helping overcome cognitive barriers. Through a variety of processes, a mediator can often help each side understand the power of the case from the other side's perspective. Moreover, by reframing the dispute and suggesting a resolution that avoids blame and stresses the positive aspects of a resolution, a mediator may be able to lessen the effects of loss aversion. . . . By emphasizing the potential gains to both sides of the resolution and de-emphasizing the losses that the resolution is going to entail, mediators (and lawyers) often facilitate resolution.

With respect to the fourth barrier, reactive devaluation, mediators can play an important and quite obvious role. Reactive devaluation can often be sidestepped if the source of a proposal is a neutral—not one of the parties. Indeed, one of the trade secrets of mediators is that after talking separately to each side about what might or might not be acceptable, the mediator takes responsibility for making a proposal. This helps both parties avoid reactive devaluation by allowing them to accept as sensible a proposal that they might have rejected if it had come directly from their adversary. . . .

Page 101.   Add Exercise 2.8 after Exercise 2.7:

EXERCISE 2.8: NAM CHOI v. AUSTIN UNIVERSITY MEDICAL SCHOOL*

Ted Nam Choi is the 23-year-old son of Cambodian immigrants who came to the United States in 1979. After graduating from Vernon Valley Community College, Nam Choi was admitted to Austin University Medical School under its affirmative action program, even though he had lower MCAT (Medical College Aptitude Test) scores than most Austin students. In view of the prestige of Austin University Medical School,

*This exercise has been adapted from an exercise developed by Thomas O. Patrick, Lecturer in Law, College of Law, West Virginia University, and is used with his permission.

one of the best in the United States, Nam Choi was thrilled to be admitted.

In December of Nam Choi's first year, however, he became aware of a difficulty in dealing with multiple choice examinations, and, by the end of the first year, he had failed five of fifteen courses. Although the Austin Medical School guidelines provide for dismissal after two course failures, the Dean, on the recommendation of the Student-Faculty Affirmative Action Committee, allowed Nam Choi to repeat the first-year program.

During the summer, Nam Choi underwent neuropsychological evaluations at the request and expense of Austin Medical School. The difficulties identified by the psychologists impair Nam Choi's ability to answer multiple choice questions. They discovered that even when he understands a subject fully and is capable of discussing it intelligently, he tends to "freeze" when forced to respond to a multiple choice question about that subject. (The psychologists suspect that this psychological blank is due to the life-or-death multiple choices that Nam Choi had to make as a child living through the fighting in Cambodia.)

Unfortunately for Nam Choi, American medical school examinations, as well as the Medical Boards which each student must pass in order to practice in the United States, are nearly all of the multiple choice type. (The exams are so designed in order to test the student's comprehension of a large body of knowledge, and capacity to make diagnostic choices.)

Nam Choi began his second exposure to the first-year program with the assistance of counseling, tutors, notetakers, and taped lectures. At the end of the year, he again failed three courses, Pharmacology, Biology, and Biochemistry. At the request of the Student-Faculty Affirmative Action Committee, the dean allowed him to take make-up exams in these courses. He failed all for the third time. Nam Choi was then dismissed from Austin Medical School.

Following an unavailing complaint with the U.S. Department of Education Office for Civil Rights, Nam Choi filed a civil action alleging that the Austin University Medical School dismissal constituted discrimination on the basis of handicap. Section 504 of the Rehabilitation Act of 1973 provides that

[n]o otherwise qualified individual with handicaps in the United States . . . shall, solely by reason of her or his handicap, be excluded from participation in, be denied the benefits of, or be subjected to discrimination under any program or activity receiving Federal financial assistance. . . .

It is undisputed that Austin University Medical School receives substantial federal financial assistance and that it is subject to the provisions of §504.

20

(Confidential information for each attorney is contained in the Teacher's Manual.)

Page 101. Add to the References:

CONDLIN, Robert J. (1992) "Bargaining in the Dark: The Normative Incoherence of Lawyer Dispute Bargaining Role," 51 *Md. L. Rev.* 1.

MNOOKIN, Robert H. (1993) "Why Negotiations Fail: An Exploration of Barriers to the Resolution of Conflict," 8 *Ohio St. J. on Disp. Resol.* 235.

MNOOKIN, Robert H., and Ronald J. GILSON (1994) "Cooperation and Conflict Between Litigators," 12 *Alternatives* 125.

MNOOKIN, Robert H., and Ronald J. GILSON (1994) "Disputing through Agents: Cooperation and Conflict Between Lawyers in Litigation," 94 *Colum. L. Rev.* 509.

SHELL, G. Richard (1991) "When Is It Legal to Lie in Negotiations?" *Sloan Mgmt. Rev.* 93 (Spring).

Chapter 3
Mediation

Page 116. *Add the following text addressing different mediation styles into the Note after the first paragraph:*

The work of Honeyman and others who have tried to synthesize common elements of effective mediation is criticized by those who hold different goals for the mediation process (Negotiation Journal, 1993). Honeyman assumes that settlement is the primary aim, but others advocate its use for personal development and interpersonal understanding rather than solely for resolving problems. Two academics supporting the latter approach, Robert A. Baruch Bush and Joseph P. Folger, state:

> [T]he mediation process contains within it a unique potential for transforming people—engendering moral growth—by helping them wrestle with difficult circumstances and bridge human differences, in the very midst of conflict. This transformative potential stems from mediation's capacity to generate two important effects, empowerment and recognition. In simplest terms, *empowerment* means the restoration to individuals of a sense of their own value and strength and their own capacity to handle life's problems. *Recognition* means the evocation in individuals of acknowledgment and empathy for the situation and problems of others. When both of these processes are held central in the practice of mediation, parties are helped to use conflicts as opportunities for moral growth, and the transformative potential of mediation is realized. [Bush and Folger, 1994: 2]

Bush and Folger advocate teaching mediation techniques that focus on supporting parties' own processes of decision-making, communication, and understanding. They suggest, for example, that the mediator ask one party to write down anything new that is learned or realized while listening to the other's opening statement. Some techniques they advocate, such as inviting the participants to ask questions arising from their genuine curiosity about each other, might seem counterproductive to a mediator intent on achieving settlement.

Deborah Kolb and Kenneth Kressel, reviewing profiles of "twelve unusually thoughtful and influential mediators," assert that mediators wedded to a particular goal often fail to meet the parties' needs for the process. Those whose techniques are designed to achieve settlement sometimes interfere with the parties' own problem-solving. Those who focus on "transformation" sometimes fail to provide the protection against bias or insult that the parties may expect (Kolb et al., 1994). Leonard Riskin suggests that mediators are predisposed by personality or background to take a particular approach to mediating. He contrasts those who view issues in mediation narrowly with those who view them broadly and those who tend to evaluate with those who tend to facilitate. Some mediators, according to Riskin, learn to modify the approach to fit the case and presumably the parties' goals for the process (Riskin, 1993).

Page 141.   Add the following new paragraphs about mediation research involving women and ethnic minorities after line 7 and before the Questions:

Researchers studying 600 small claims cases in New Mexico concluded that women who are claimants achieved the same or better (the same if claimants, better if respondents) monetary success in mediation relative to men. Ethnic minority parties (87 percent Hispanic), however, fared worse monetarily in mediation, unless the co-mediators were both ethnic minorities. Ethnic minority parties also fared worse in litigation, but still did better in adjudication than in mediation (Hermann, LaFree, Rack, and West, 1993). Co-researcher Michele Hermann, a law professor at the University of New Mexico, warns that further analysis of the data is needed before concluding that ethnicity or gender alone explains these results. At the same time, Professor Hermann argues that those running mediation programs should "pay serious attention to the potential impact of power imbalances . . ." (Hermann, 1994).

Over half of the parties in the New Mexico study had lawyers (Hermann, 1994), but ethnic minorities were less likely to be represented by counsel. For a discussion of the effect of legal representation on the fairness of the mediation process, see McEwen and Rogers, 1994, Supplement, Chapter 7, p. 62.

Page 156.   Regarding lines 3-5 and the last full paragraph:

See Supplement additions to page 141 suggesting that men and women may experience dispute resolution processes differently and outcomes may be tied to both ethnicity of mediator and of parties.

*Page 171.   Add the following new paragraph before the
             Questions:*

The 1994 SPIDR Qualifications Commission Draft Report reaffirmed the 1989 Commission's view that knowledge about what constitutes "competency" for a mediator and other types of neutrals is "at a nascent stage." The commission pointed out that desirable abilities for the neutral might vary depending on the aims for the dispute resolution process and the setting and parties. Given these contextual variations, the commission recommended against mediator licensure and urged those who might impose qualifications not to restrict unnecessarily either party choice or the diversity of the mediator pool. See also Margaret Shaw, "Selection, Training and Qualifications of Neutrals," in Keilitz (1993).

*Page 177.   Add the following new paragraphs addressing
             mediator immunity before the Questions:*

The U.S. Court of Appeals for the District of Columbia recently ruled that court-appointed case evaluators (a term the court says can be used interchangeably with mediators) were entitled to quasi-judicial immunity. *Wagshal v. Foster,* 28 F.3d 1249 (D.C. Cir. 1994). See also *Meyers v. Contra Costa County Department of Social Services,* 812 F.2d 1154 (9th Cir. 1987), *cert. denied,* 484 U.S. 829 (1987) (court employees acting as conciliators entitled to quasi-judicial immunity). The *Wagshal* court pointed out the similarity of case evaluation to judicial case management and settlement activities and stated that the aggrieved party had adequate remedies without recourse to civil liability. The adequacy of other remedies is questioned by a new set of standards. The National Standards for Court-Connected Mediation Programs (Center for Dispute Settlement, 1992) warn against extending immunity to mediators, reasoning that it is inappropriate to deny "recourse to litigants injured by incompetent service," especially if the service is provided for a fee (p. 14-2).

If mediators are immune from liability, what relief is available if the mediator makes statements to the judge that might prejudice a party's case or discloses information when confidentiality has been promised? Should relief be available? Should it matter whether the mediator is appointed by a court or charges a fee?

Page 184.   Add to the end of Question 3.22:

In recent cases, parties seeking to enforce an oral agreement reached in mediation were precluded from introducing evidence because of mediation privilege statutes. *Hudson v. Hudson,* 600 So.2d 7 (Fla. App. 1992); *Ryan v. Garcia,* 27 Cal. App. 4th 1006 (Ct. App. 1994). See also *Bennett v. Bennett,* 587 A.2d 463 (Me. Sup. Ct. 1991) (not a violation of good faith mediation requirement to refuse to execute an agreement reached in mediation, noting that otherwise conversations within mediation session would have to be disclosed). Should the mediator be required to warn the parties to a privileged mediation that their agreement will not be enforceable until reduced to writing?

Page 190.   *After Question 3.31 add Questions 3.32, 3.33, and 3.34:*

3.32   Mr. O'Leary, a retired minister and volunteer mediator in a community mediation center, opened each mediation with a statement that the session was confidential. After a mediation between Mrs. George and her landlord, Mr. O'Leary reported to the public children's services agency that he had heard Mrs. George admit to leaving her young children unsupervised for long periods of time. He said that he feared for the children's safety. Mrs. George was charged with child neglect. Later she sued Mr. O'Leary for breach of the promised confidentiality and for mediator malpractice. Mr. O'Leary was not obligated by statute to report child neglect, though a state statute required physicians, social workers, and teachers to report child abuse. Should Mr. O'Leary be exempt from liability because he was a volunteer and was acting to protect children from harm?

3.33   Subsequent to the suit described in 3.32, the mediators at the community mediation center decided to stop promising confidentiality. In fact, they began each mediation with the statement, "We can typically keep what is said during a mediation session confidential but occasionally we hear something that we believe, in good conscience, must be reported to the authorities. Therefore, we cannot guarantee complete confidentiality regarding what is said here today." Thereafter, they reported to public authorities in cases ranging from the dumping of toxic chemicals to probable child neglect. Suppose the code of ethics in Appendix B, p. 475 of the casebook, applies to the mediators. Have the mediators acted unethically? Should it be unethical for mediators to disclaim broad confidentiality? What should a code of ethics for mediators require with respect to confidentiality?

3.34   Acme, Inc. and Widgets Unlimited entered into a supply contract containing the clause, "We agree that, prior to filing litigation, we will mediate in good faith any disputes arising under this contract." During the mediation of a dispute concerning the first widget shipment sent to Acme, Acme's lawyer and president refused to say anything except, "We'll see you in court." Naturally the case did not settle in mediation, and Acme sued. When Widgets sought to introduce evidence of Acme's statements during the mediation session in order to prove breach of the clause requiring good faith mediation (see Katz, p. 442 of the casebook), Acme's lawyer objected on the basis of the state's mediation privilege statute. The court sustained the objection. Should the privilege statute be amended to permit evidence relevant to enforcement of a good faith mediation clause? Can mediation clauses be effective in the absence of such an amendment? Compare Question 6.12, p. 276 of the casebook, and the Sherman article, p. 48 of this Supplement.

Page 190.   Before the Mediation Exercises add the following new section, which includes an article and Question 3.35:

E.   THE ROLE OF LAWYERS IN MEDIATION PROCEEDINGS

M. LEWIS, ADVOCACY IN MEDIATION: ONE MEDIATOR'S VIEW*

Disp. Resol. Mag. (forthcoming, Fall 1995)

In the past two years, there has been a growing literature on representing parties in mediation. That literature probably reflects the increasing use of mediation by individual litigants and by state and federal trial courts. One hopes that the increase also reflects a growing realization that mediation is different from direct lawyer negotiation or the negotiations that often take place as a case approaches trial. In understanding those differences, a lawyer's representation of a client in mediation can help the client achieve her goals. Failure to understand the differences can doom lawyer and client to reach an agreement that is less than optimal, or hinder reaching any agreement at all.

To discuss fully the role of an advocate in mediation, it might be useful to explore briefly the stages a mediation moves through. All mediations that do not terminate prematurely will move through four stages: *gathering information* on the dispute, *developing possible options* for

*This article, written by Michael Lewis, will appear in Dispute Resolution Magazine, Fall 1995.

resolving the problem, getting the parties to *choose from among the various options* available for consideration and *closure*. Throughout the process the mediator will be focused on helping the parties achieve a resolution of the dispute acceptable to all.

Clearly, the first point at which representation is important comes at the stage at which lawyer and client meet to discuss which dispute resolution process offers the best hopes of realizing the client's interests or needs. This article assumes that that discussion has taken place, and that together lawyer and client have chosen mediation. Lawyer and client must then prepare for the mediation—a point at which an advocate's help and advice are critical to future success. . . .

Preparation for mediation requires a discussion of the client's needs—and some discussion of what the needs of the other party to the dispute might be. Clearly, the second phase of this discussion will be based on imperfect knowledge. It is important, however, for lawyer and client to engage in the discussion, since if they focus on the other side's interests and likely goals, they may well be able to think through possible solutions to meet the other side's needs and yet achieve what they need out of the mediation.

For advocates representing institutional clients, one of the issues to be discussed should be that of who from among the possible institutional representatives should participate in the mediation. Much is made of the question of authority at the mediation table—that is, can the representative at the table commit the institution to an agreement? While important, this mediator believes that the question of participation in the mediation often is a balancing act, with the criteria of authority to bind, in-depth knowledge necessary to craft an optimal agreement, ability to communicate to the other side and an ability to empathize with the other side all important in the decision.

There are times when a company might want to have most involved in the mediation the person who best knows the aspect of the business in dispute. In others, the person with the most personal and direct knowledge about a dispute might not be the best company representative. Employment disputes are a good example of the latter. In those disputes, the person from the company with the most thorough knowledge of the dispute often is the person most complained about by the employee. In that situation, involvement of that particular representative might doom the mediation to a series of charges and counter-charges generating a great deal of heat and very little light.

At the mediation session, the mediator quickly will move to generating the information necessary to help the parties move towards an agreement. It is at this stage of the mediation that counsel plays a second pivotal role. Trial lawyers are accustomed to negotiating directly with lawyers on the other side of cases. They are less accustomed to having an unfettered opportunity to make a pitch to the principals on the other side. A critical early question for lawyer and client should be how to make the best possible presentation to those principals. Should the lawyer (or client) go for the jugular, or should the approach be one designed to encourage the other side to begin thinking about possible ways of resolving the dispute through mediation? The answer seems self-evident, but it is a common failing of advocates in mediation that they seem to forget that the most important figure in the room is not the mediator but the principal (and lawyer) for the opposition.

Thus, the opening presentations often need to walk a tightrope between focusing on achieving a settlement in the mediation without appearing to discard the possibility of litigating to the hilt if that becomes necessary. The parties often are attempting to educate the mediator in the early stages of the process. Demonstrative evidence can sometimes prove to be a powerful tool. A chart, outlining the chronology of a series of transactions can be helpful. Linda Singer, a well-known mediator, recently described the use by an advocate of a series of videotaped excerpts from depositions of the other side's managers. To the supervisor who had not been party to the depositions, and who had been assured that they had gone well, the videotape was a powerful convincer. The advent of computer technology means that advocates can produce (or ask their client to produce) presentations such as spreadsheets which can provide a powerful analytic tool for use at the mediation table.

Whatever the vehicle—charts, videotapes, spreadsheets—the emphasis should be on presenting a cohesive theme or story as economically as possible. I recently sat through a 2½ hour opening presentation by a lawyer in a complicated case. The opening was less persuasive than it should have been because it went on too long, and instead of "hooking" the other side into thinking about settlement, it bored them and they appeared to think about little during most of the presentation.

As pointed out above, one important difference between most lawyer negotiations and mediation is that clients are expected to take an active role in fashioning solutions in mediations. That fact, coupled with the fact that parties can expect to meet with the mediator separately, presents both opportunities and potential pitfalls. If clients are present during mediation sessions, most mediators will expect the client to speak—to offer her perspectives on the dispute and what her interests are. A lawyer unprepared for the series of questions aimed at her client by the mediator may be inclined simply to interpose herself between client and mediator. This reaction carries with it two burdens: one substantive, the second practical.

The substantive burden that barring the mediator from talking directly with her client carries with it is that if the mediator is armed with imperfect knowledge about what is most important to the client, she is hampered in her ability to help achieve those goals. The practical burden on the lawyer also is considerable. Most mediators, at least in meetings with one side to a dispute, will not permit the lawyer to interpose herself without some struggle. Generally conducted wearing velvet gloves (at least on the mediator's part) this struggle between mediator and lawyer is one that the lawyer can win only rarely. After all, her client wants to talk about the problem, and any available offer to understand and help is welcome.

Most mediators meet with parties in a combination of joint and separate meetings. It is important for lawyers to understand the differences between these sessions, what the mediator may be trying to accomplish and what she and her client should be seeking. The initial joint meeting provides the lawyer and client an opportunity to speak directly to the other principal(s) involved in the mediation. While few mediators would suggest that the lawyer and client put on a presentation that is so polished that it seems canned, failure to plan adequately for this session can miss a major opportunity to make a presentation to the principals on the other side.

If the mediator intends to spend time with the parties in separate sessions, it is important for advocates to make sure they understand the extent of the confidentiality to be offered by the mediator in those sessions. A good place to start here is by looking at the jurisdiction's statute (if there is one) on mediator confidentiality. There are currently many such statutes. If the mediation is taking place under the auspices of a court program, the advocate should review the rules governing the program, as many of them have rules on confidentiality. Most mediators in private practice have developed agreements to mediate explicitly establishing the mediator's offer of confidentiality to the parties. Some court programs forbid mediators from using such agreements, so it is important for advocates to establish the scope of confidentiality protections applicable in their particular mediation.

If the advocate is assured about confidentiality protections, then she should consider how best to use the mediator in the early stages of the mediation. In these sessions, the mediator is likely to be interested in any sensitive information that the client and advocate might want to share with the mediator but not with the other side. This information may be of two kinds—sensitive information about what happened in the transaction or dispute, and information regarding the client's real needs—or interests—in the mediation. Here, the advocate is likely to face a mediator who probes—either gently or not, depending on the mediator's style—what the advocate and her client have said in the joint session. From the mediator's point of view the exploration is designed to equip her with additional information that might be useful in helping the parties fashion an agreement. An advocate who attempts to thwart this exploration, by, for example, continuing to interpose herself between the mediator and her client, runs the risk of missing an opportunity. The advocate who embraces the mediator and tries to use her as an ally, on the other hand, begins to maximize what may be possible in the mediation.

Is it folly to speak of the mediator as ally? In the traditional sense, perhaps. The late James Laue, a prominent mediator, especially in public policy disputes, used to say that the mediator is an "advocate for the process." Jim meant that a mediator could not afford to be perceived as an advocate for one of the parties over another, but that a mediator trusted by the parties would learn sensitive information that might provide the key to an ultimate resolution of the dispute. If the advocate can view the mediator as an ally to all of the parties to the dispute, she may be willing to share the kind of information that helps the mediator work with all of the parties towards a settlement.

How might the advocate use the mediator as an ally? First, as suggested above, the advocate and client may want to share sensitive information about the details of the dispute and possible acceptable outcomes. Second, the advocate and client should think through how they want to explore settlement possibilities with the other side. Obviously, the dilemma the advocate faces here is protecting her client against overreaching by the other side. If Side A understands that Side B is willing to accept a particularly favorable (to Side A) settlement, there is little incentive to offer more. The mediator may be able to discuss settlement alternatives with Side A without conveying necessarily that Side B would find such alternatives acceptable.

Given that most mediations involve a series of meetings with the mediator, it is important for advocates to use "down time," that is time when the mediator is meeting with the other side, to consider any information the mediator may have conveyed about the other side, and to plan further with her client. If the information conveyed suggests new settlement possibilities, thinking this through with the client may open the door for a settlement that better meets the interests of the client. If the information conveyed suggests that the other side is proceeding in a way likely to generate a series of unacceptable settlement possibilities, the sooner the mediator understands this the better.

Finally, given the fluid nature of many mediations, lawyer and client may be presented with settlement possibilities that had not been considered at the outset. The advocate should be careful not to reject these possibilities too quickly, and to discuss them with the client as carefully as possible given the client's interests in the dispute. It is not uncommon for clients to disclose new interests in the course of a mediation, or to change the priority order among a number of important interests. If this happens, the advocate should discuss any settlement possibilities in light of newly disclosed interests or changed priorities.

Towards the end of the mediation, the choice for the client may well be between a potential agreement meeting most of the client's interests or resolving the dispute through litigation; only rarely will she be offered what she said at the outset she wanted. If the advocate believes that one or more of the possible settlements meets all of the essential needs of the client, and that those needs are unlikely to be met through any other forum at an acceptable cost, the mediator may be a useful ally.

In these discussions, the mediator will attempt to keep both advocate and client focused on interests—those issues that go to the heart of the client's concern about this case. A good mediator will not permit a party (or advocate) to assert simply that she wants something. The mediator will return again and again to what the client and advocate have stated are the core interests, and lead them through an analysis of whether those core interests are met by the various settlement possibilities. Those that do not will be discarded, at least for the moment. The mediator's focus will be on those settlement possibilities that appear to meet the announced interests.

In all of these discussions, the mediator will make it clear that the client must make the final decision about accepting a settlement. An advocate who believes that her client is unreasonably rejecting settlement possibilities that might resolve the dispute while meeting the client's articulated needs, can use the mediator to help make the necessary points with the client without running the risk of having useful advice rejected out of stubbornness or a misplaced sense of what is likely to happen at trial. A good mediator will pick up signals from an advocate that she believes her client is not acting out of her own self-interest. The mediator can be encouraged to explore the issues of interests, whether the possible settlement meets those interests, and what the likely litigation outcomes might be in a manner that provides the maximum amount of freedom for the client's decision, but assures as much as possible that whatever decision the client makes will be an informed one.

Fundamentally, many mediators will focus on helping the parties in a dispute achieve as many of their goals as can be reconciled. The advocate should not fight with the mediator for the heart and mind of the client. Rather, the advocate should help the mediator understand

that heart and mind so that she can more fully provide the assistance
that a good mediator can bring to the parties' negotiation.

Questions

3.35 As Michael Lewis intimates in his title, these are a mediator's
views of the role of a representative lawyer in mediation. How, if at all,
might those views differ if your perspective were that of the lawyer?

Page 195.   Add Exercise 3.9 after Exercise 3.8:

EXERCISE 3.9: PROSANDO V. HIGH-TECH*

Prosando, a German-Argentine joint venture based in Argentina, is
a distributor of office and business equipment. High-Tech is a large, well-
established computer manufacturer, with its headquarters in southern
California.

In January 1990, Prosando entered into an exclusive five-year distribution contract with High-Tech. Prosando agreed to establish a distribution network for High-Tech's Futura A and B minicomputers
throughout South America and to use High-Tech's trademark in
doing so.

Immediately after the contract was signed, Prosando ordered 50
Futura A computers. High-Tech, however, refused to ship until its legal
department had reviewed the contract. Following that review, in June
1990, High-Tech insisted that it retain the right to sell directly in South
America. Prosando reluctantly agreed, and in August 1990, High-Tech
shipped 50 Futura A computers to Prosando.

In October 1990, Prosando ordered another 20 Futura A computers,
which were delivered in December 1990. In January 1991, High-Tech
discontinued the Futura A and introduced the Century series, but refused initially to allow Prosando to distribute that series. According to
High-Tech, Prosando's distribution contract was limited to the Futura
series. In June 1991 (one and one-half years into the contract), High-

---

*This exercise was created for the CPR Institute for Dispute Resolution by Cathy
Cronin-Harris, Vice President, and Professor Stephen Goldberg as a basis for CPR's 36-
minute videotape, *Mediation in Action: Resolving a Complex Business Dispute* (1994). The
videotape is available from CPR, 366 Madison Avenue, 14th floor, New York, NY 10017
(212)949-6490. Copyright © 1994 by the CPR Institute for Dispute Resolution. Reprinted
with the permission of CPR.

Tech agreed to allow Prosando to distribute the Century series. In February 1992, Prosando ordered 18 Century series computers.

In June 1992, without prior warning, High-Tech notified Prosando that the contract would be terminated in 30 days because of Prosando's clear and unequivocal breach of contract. According to High-Tech, Prosando had:

1. Failed to use its best efforts to sell the product within the assigned territory to the total dissatisfaction of the Seller, since Prosando had placed orders for only 88 units of product in 24 months.
2. Failed to establish a "distributor" network on or before June 30, 1991. As of June 1992, Prosando had established a total of four distributors, all in Chile.
3. Failed to submit or negotiate annual purchase commitments.

The relevant provisions of the contract are these:

A. Prosando shall have the sole right (except for High-Tech) to sell High-Tech Futura A and Futura B minicomputers, and any updates thereto (hereafter "the product") within the assigned territory.
B. Prosando shall use its best efforts to sell within the assigned territory.
C. Prosando shall establish a distribution network within the assigned territory to the satisfaction of High-Tech.
D. Prosando shall have its distribution network in place by June 1991. If it fails to do so, High-Tech shall have the right to terminate Prosando's status as exclusive South American distributor of the product, and to engage other distributors in addition to Prosando.
E. Prosando must place a noncancellable blanket order for 100 of the product totalling one million U.S. dollars upon execution of this agreement for delivery on or after _____ . (Left blank in the contract.)
F. On each calendar year commencing in _____ (left blank in the contract) the parties will agree on the minimum purchase requirements for the subsequent twelve-month period. If agreement is not achieved, either party may terminate this agreement upon prior 90 days' written notice.
G. Upon termination of this Agreement becoming effective: (a) Neither party shall be liable to the other for loss of profits or prospective profits of any kind or nature sustained or arising out of or alleged to have arisen out of such termination.

On receiving High-Tech's June 1992 notice of termination, Prosando continued to sell its remaining High-Tech equipment.

In September 1992, Prosando initiated litigation in the U.S. District Court for the Southern District of California, claiming damages for breach of contract and fraud: $1 million for loss of business reputation; $6 million for lost profits; and actual reliance damages of $3 million expended on the contract (including capitalized loans, leasing of premises, personnel, promoting and advertising the product, travel, etc.), a total of $10 million.

High-Tech denied all allegations and counterclaimed for $126,000 for equipment shipped and not paid for.

At the suggestion of the district court, the parties have agreed to attempt to resolve this dispute through mediation.

(Confidential information for attorneys and business executives is contained in the Teacher's Manual.)

Page 195.   Add the following to the References:

BUSH, Robert A. Baruch (1994) "Symposium: Dilemmas of Mediation Practice," *J. Disp. Resol.* 1.

BUSH, Robert A. Baruch, and Joseph P. FOLGER (1994) *The Promise of Mediation.* San Francisco: Jossey-Bass.

CENTER FOR DISPUTE SETTLEMENT (1992) *National Standards for Court-Connected Mediation Programs.* Washington, D.C.: CDS.

GIBSON, Kevin V. (1992) "Confidentiality in Mediation: A Moral Reassessment," *J. Disp. Resol.* 25.

HERMANN, Michele (1994) "New Mexico Research Examines Impact of Gender and Ethnicity in Mediation," *Disp. Resol. Mag.* 10 (Fall).

HERMANN, Michele, Gary LAFREE, Christine RACK, and Mary Beth WEST (1993) *The Metrocourt Project Final Report.* Albuquerque: University of New Mexico Center for the Study and Resolution of Disputes.

KEILITZ, Susan (1993) *National Symposium on Court-Connected Dispute Resolution Research.* Williamsburg: National Center for State Courts.

KOLB, Deborah M., and Associates (1994) *When Talk Works: Profiles of Mediators.* San Francisco: Jossey-Bass.

KOVACH, Kimberlee (1994) *Mediation: Principles and Practice.* St. Paul: West.

LEWIS, Michael (forthcoming) "Advocacy in Mediation: One Mediator's View," *Disp. Resol. Mag.* (Fall 1995).

NEGOTIATION JOURNAL (1993) "Who Really Is a Mediator? A Special Section on the Interim Guidelines," Vol. 9, p. 290.

RISKIN, Leonard (1993) "Mediator Orientations, Strategies and Techniques," *Alternatives* 111 (Sept.).

ROGERS, Nancy H., and Craig A. MCEWEN (1994) *Mediation: Law, Policy, Practice, 2d ed.* New York: Clark Boardman Callaghan.

SINGER, Linda R. (1994) *Settling Disputes: Conflict Resolution in Business, Families, and the Legal System, 2d ed.* Boulder: Westview.
SOCIETY OF PROFESSIONALS IN DISPUTE RESOLUTION (1994) *Ensuring Competence and Quality in Dispute Resolution* (draft report of the Commission on Qualifications).

Chapter 4
Arbitration

Page 217.   Insert the following Notes and report at the bottom of the page:

Note: Post-Gilmer Developments

The judicial, scholarly, and public reaction to *Gilmer* and its predecessors has been predominantly negative. According to critics of these decisions, their effect is to allow the more powerful party to a relationship to impose arbitration on the weaker, and so vitiate congressional intention to provide statutory protection for the latter. This charge has been brought with particular vehemence by those who view employees as being stripped of the protection of civil rights statutes by employers who insist as a condition of employment that employees agree to arbitrate all claims against their employer, including those arising out of alleged statutory violations (see, e.g., *Prudential Ins. Co. v. Lai*, 42 F.3d 1299 (9th Cir. 1994); and see generally Gorman (forthcoming)).

One response to these criticisms has been the introduction of a number of bills in Congress that would bar enforcement of employer-employee agreements to arbitrate statutorily based discrimination claims unless the agreement was entered into after the dispute arose. Another response was provided by President Clinton's Commission on the Future of Worker-Management Relationships (generally known as the "Dunlop Commission," chaired by former U.S. Secretary of Labor John Dunlop). The Dunlop Commission carefully analyzed the strengths and weaknesses of both litigation and arbitration in enforcing employee antidiscrimination claims before concluding that arbitration, even if it contains "the quality standards necessary to ensure effective protection of employees' substantive legal rights," should not be legally enforceable if entered into before a dispute has arisen.

As you read the following excerpts from the Dunlop Commission's report, consider whether the Commission's conclusion is consistent with its analysis.

COMMISSION ON THE FUTURE OF WORKER-MANAGEMENT RELATIONS, REPORT AND RECOMMENDATIONS

25–33 (1994)

[E]mployment litigation has spiraled in the last two decades. The expansion of federal and state discrimination laws and the growth in common law and statutory protection against wrongful dismissal have provided employees with a broader array of tools with which to challenge employer behavior in court. In the federal courts alone, the number of suits filed concerning employment grievances grew over 400 percent in the last two decades. Complaints lodged with administrative agencies have risen at a similar rate: for example, in 1993, the EEOC received nearly 90,000 discrimination complaints from employees across the country.

Employment litigation is a costly option for both employers and employees. For every dollar paid to employees through litigation, at least another dollar is paid to attorneys involved in handling both meritorious and non-meritorious claims. Moreover, aside from the direct costs of litigation, employers often dedicate significant sums to designing defensive personnel practices (with the help of lawyers) to minimize their litigation exposure. These costs tend to affect compensation: as the firm's employment law expenses grow, less resources are available to provide wage and benefits to workers.

Further, while the prospective costs of court awards do serve to deter employers from illegal actions, it is not clear that litigation protects all kinds of employees equally well. Most employment discrimination suits are brought by employees who have already left the job where the discrimination took place. Further, those ex-employees who bring suit tend to come from the ranks of managers and professionals rather than from lower-level workers.

Finally, even for those employees properly situated to file suit, the pursuit of a legal claim through litigation often proves stressful and unsatisfying. Overburdened federal and state judicial dockets mean that years often pass before an aggrieved employee is able to present his or her claim in court. The combative nature of litigation tends to push the employee to the sidelines in this legal struggle, though occasionally subjecting employees to detailed investigation of their personal histories and character.

These problems with the legislative model have led many employers, employee groups, and lawmakers to seek alternatives. In fact, in both the Americans with Disabilities Act of 1990 and the Civil Rights Act of 1991, Congress specifically encouraged alternative methods of resolving

discrimination disputes "where appropriate and to the extent authorized by the law." . . .

In 1991, the United States Supreme Court showed itself receptive
to the arbitration model of binding ADR mechanisms. In its *Gilmer*
decision, . . . the Court enforced a securities dealer's agreement to
arbitrate all disputes, including employment disputes arising under
public laws (there, age discrimination). It is important to note, however,
that the Supreme Court in *Gilmer* did not specifically address whether
employers generally could require arbitration under the employment
contract. The Commission also underlines that the Court's decision
rested on an interpretation of the Federal Arbitration Act (FAA)—a
statute enacted in 1920, more than forty years before modern employment rights were created.

The Supreme Court . . . assumed in *Gilmer* that arbitration
agreements were enforceable only if the arbitration system satisfied
minimum standards of quality. The court did not, however, conduct a
systematic appraisal of the problems posed by integrating arbitration
into the employment setting, nor did it issue any specific guidelines for
judicial review of arbitral design.

Testimony before the Commission indicated that recent employer
experimentation with arbitration has produced programs that range
from serious and fair alternatives to litigation, to mechanisms that appear to be of dubious merit for enforcing the public values embedded
in our laws.[3] The challenge, then, is how to encourage the creative
potential of alternatives to standard court litigation, while ensuring that
the legal needs and priorities of a diverse American work force are
fairly satisfied. . . .

. . . [T]he Commission believes that development of private arbitration alternatives for workplace disputes must be encouraged. High-
quality alternatives to litigation hold the promise of expanding access
to public law rights for lower-wage workers. Private arbitration may also
allow even the most contentious disputes to be resolved in a manner
which permits the complaining employee to raise the dispute without
permanently fracturing the employee's working relationship with the
employer.

In light of the important social values embodied in public employ-

---

3. A Wall Street Journal article ("More Law Firms Seek Arbitration for Internal
Disputes," Sept. 26, 1994, p. B 13) describes how a number of large law firms are
establishing ADR programs in the wake of a $7 million jury verdict against a firm for
sexual harassment by one of its partners. One of the programs mentioned was troubling:
the arbitrator for an employee's dispute had to be selected from a pool composed of
partners in law firms with 50 lawyers or more.

ment law and regulation, however, the Commission believes that a shift to private alternatives must proceed carefully. Significant quality standards should be met by the private arbitration mechanisms developed by individual firms and their employees, to enhance the contributions they make to insuring both protection of and respect for America's workforce. . . .

. . . In specific terms, the Commission recommends the following guide posts for ensuring quality in private arbitration:

Selection of arbitrator. The selection process should allow both the employer and the affected employee(s) to participate. The arbitrator should be selected from a roster of qualified arbitrators who have training and experience in the area of law disputed and are certified by professional associations specializing in such dispute resolution. Attention should be paid to ensuring that professional rosters include women and minorities in significant numbers. Neither party should be able to limit the roster unilaterally so as to risk the possibility that the arbitrator finally selected will be biased in favor of that side.

Procedures. Aggrieved employees should have the opportunity to gather the relevant information they need to support their legal claims. Employees pursuing a claim, for example, should be granted access to their personnel files. Broader access to personnel files should also be available for workers bringing disparate impact or treatment claims. Workplace arbitration systems might also consider allowing a complaining employee at least one deposition, or official interview, of a company official of the employee's choosing. The arbitrator should be empowered to expand discovery to include any material he or she finds valuable for resolving the dispute.

Payment of arbitrator. To ensure impartiality of the arbitrator, both the employee and the employer should contribute to the arbitrator's fee. Ideally, the employee contribution should be capped in proportion to the employee's pay, so as to avoid discouraging claims by lower-wage workers.

Awards and remedies. The introduction of a workplace arbitration system should not curb substantive employee protections. This means that private arbitration must offer employees the same array of remedies available to them through litigation in court. Public law arbitrators should be empowered to award whatever relief—including reinstatement, back pay, additional economic damages, punitive awards, injunctive relief, and attorney's fees—that would be available in court under the law in question.

Final arbitrator ruling. The arbitrator should issue a written opinion spelling out the findings of fact and reasons which led to the decision. This opinion need not correspond in style or length to a court opinion. However, it should set out in understandable terms the basis for the arbitrator's ruling.

Court review. Judicial review of arbitrator rulings must ensure that the arbitration decision reflects an appropriate understanding and interpretation of the relevant legal doctrines. While a reviewing court should defer to an arbitrator's fact findings as long as they have substantial evidentiary basis, the reviewing court's authoritative interpretation of the law should bind arbitrators as much it now binds administrative agencies and lower courts. For example, if an arbitration decision in regard to a sexual harassment claim fails to grasp and apply the standard set for such claims by the Supreme Court, the reviewing court must overturn the arbitration decision as inconsistent with current law. . . .

Having set out the key requirements for high-quality arbitration, the Commission now turns to the question of whether—with respect to an arbitration system which satisfies the quality standards listed above—an employee's agreement to arbitrate an employment law claim should be legally enforceable. Growing out of the *Gilmer* decision, the Commission recognizes, is a major debate over whether an employee may agree, as a condition of employment, to be bound by an employer's arbitration system. . . .

The public rights embodied in state and federal employment law—such as freedom from discrimination in the workplace and minimum wage and overtime standards—are an important part of the social and economic protections of the nation. Employees required to accept binding arbitration of such disputes would face what for many would be an inappropriate choice: give up your right to go to court, or give up your job. Private arbitration systems, which we believe can work well if properly administered, will have to prove themselves through experience before the nation is in a position to decide whether employers should be allowed to require their employees to use them as a condition of employment. We urge employers to experiment broadly with voluntary programs so the nation can gain experience with this potentially valuable tool. . . .

Binding arbitration agreements should not be enforceable as a condition of employment. The Commission believes the courts should interpret the Federal Arbitration Act in this fashion. If they fail to do,

Congress should pass legislation making it clear that any choice between available methods for enforcing statutory employment rights should be left to the individual who feels wronged rather than dictated by his or her employment contract. At some time in the future, as the nation gains experience with private arbitration systems, it may wish to reevaluate the situation. . . .

The Commission encourages employees whose employers offer arbitration programs that meet the standards outlined above to consider their use when a dispute occurs. Employees who decide to use a private arbitration system instead of going to court after a dispute over a legal right has arisen should be bound by the results of the arbitration decision subject to the limited court review we specified above.

Note

Although the *Gilmer* case involved an employment discrimination claim under a federal statute, its encouragement of predispute arbitration clauses has had far-reaching ramifications. Perhaps the most notable extension has been in the consumer area. In 1993, the Bank of America notified all of its retail deposit customers as well as its credit card customers that henceforth all individual disputes between customers and the bank would be resolved by final and binding arbitration to be administered by the American Arbitration Association. Class actions would be handled by reference under California Code of Civil Procedure §638 (see casebook, p. 291). In neither case could trial by jury be had.

This scheme was upheld in *Badie v. Bank of America,* No. 944916, 1994 WL 660730 (Cal. App. Dept. Super. Ct. Aug. 18, 1994). The court concluded that although this contract was clearly a contract of adhesion, it was not unconscionable since the affected customers could withdraw their business and go elsewhere and since the designated procedures were not shown to be inherently unfair (see Dispute Resolution Magazine, 1994). See generally Budnitz (1995).

Page 221. Add to the References:

BUDNITZ, Mark (1995) "Arbitration of Disputes Between Consumers and Financial Institutions: A Serious Threat to Consumer Protection," 10 *Ohio St. J. on Disp. Resol.* 267.
COMMISSION ON THE FUTURE OF WORKER-MANAGEMENT RELA-

TIONS (1994) Report and Recommendations. Washington D.C.: Government Printing Office.

DISPUTE RESOLUTION MAGAZINE (1994) "Face Off: Should Binding Arbitration Clauses Be Prohibited in Consumer Contracts?" (Summer), p. 4.

GORMAN, Robert A. (forthcoming) "The *Gilmer* Decision and the Private Arbitration of Public Law Disputes," *U. Ill. L. Rev.* (June 1995)

MACNEIL, Ian (1992) *American Arbitration Law.* Boston: Little, Brown.

MACNEIL, Ian, Richard SPEIDEL, and Thomas STIPANOWICH (1994) *Federal Arbitration Law: Agreements, Awards, and Remedies Under the Federal Arbitration Act.* Boston: Little, Brown.

Chapter 5

Hybrid Processes

Page 230.   Add Exercise 5.0 after the carry-over paragraph:

EXERCISE 5.0: SOUTHERN ELECTRIC COMPANY AND
              PUBLIC UTILITY WORKERS UNION,
              AFL-CIO*

Southern Electric is a public utility serving four Southern and Central states. Its 10,000 service, maintenance and clerical employees are represented by the Public Utility Workers Union, AFL-CIO.

The collective bargaining agreement, in addition to the typical management rights clause and provision for discipline for just cause, allows the Company to establish reasonable rules concerning the conduct of employees. Under the latter provision, the Company, for the last four years, has had a rule providing for the discharge of any employee, who, in the course of operating Company vehicles, is involved in three preventable accidents in a three-year period. This rule is contained in the Employee Handbook provided to all employees when they are hired, and is posted in areas used by employees with vehicle operating responsibilities. Prior to this case, no employee had reached the three accident-three year level. Nor has the Union ever challenged the reasonableness of the three accident-three year rule.

The Company has a comprehensive safety program for all drivers, including a 20-hour defensive driving course for employees newly assigned to Company vehicles. The Safety Department conducts these courses; it also investigates all accidents involving Company vehicles. Any employee found by the Safety Department to have been involved in a preventable accident must repeat the defensive driving course.

Joe Doaks has ten years of service with the Company. For three years

*This mediation simulation was developed by Mediation Research & Education Project, Inc., Northwestern University Law School, 357 East Chicago Avenue, Chicago, IL 60611, and is reprinted with permission. A videotape of the mediation is available from Mediation Research & Education Project, Inc.

he was a maintenance mechanic in the shop, repairing and maintaining equipment. For the last seven years, he has been a maintenance driver, operating out of a Company truck to perform maintenance and repair work on fixed equipment.

Nine months ago, Doaks was involved in an accident while driving a Company truck. The official Safety Department accident report stated that an automobile approaching Doaks' truck, on the opposite side of a two-lane road, had turned left in front of Doaks' truck, that Doaks swerved and braked to avoid colliding with the auto, but hit the right front fender of the auto, causing approximately $500 damage to each vehicle. The report went on to state that Doaks could have avoided the accident had he practiced defensive driving techniques.

The police report stated that Doaks' skid marks indicated he was observing the 25 mile per hour speed limit; that the weather was clear and that visibility was normal. It quoted the driver of the other car as saying that she signaled before she turned in front of Doaks' truck, and quoted Doaks as denying that she had signaled. Neither driver was charged by the police with having violated traffic laws.

Doaks had been involved in two previous accidents while driving Company vehicles within the past three years, both of which had been found preventable. One, two years ago, was relatively minor. The other, approximately eighteen months ago, had resulted in an out-of-court settlement by the Company of $40,000. After each of these accidents Doaks repeated the defensive driving course, but received no discipline. The Union did not file a grievance in either instance.

Based on the Safety Department's report of the most recent accident, and on the previous two preventable accidents, the Company discharged Doaks at a meeting at which Doaks had Union representation. Within the contract's time limits he filed a grievance for reinstatement with full back pay. The grievance was not resolved at the first three steps of the grievance procedure, and is now scheduled for mediation. If the grievance is not resolved at mediation, the Union has the contractual right to demand final and binding arbitration.

(Confidential information for the mediator, the grievant, the Union representative, the Company maintenance superintendent, and the Company industrial relations manager is contained in the Teacher's Manual.)

Page 239.   Add to the References:

METZLOFF, Thomas (1992) "Reconfiguring the Summary Jury Trial," 41 *Duke L.J.* 806.

Chapter 6

Dispute Resolution in the Justice System

Page 249. *At the end of the last paragraph at the bottom of the page, add the following sentence:*

[See Marc Galanter and Mia Cahill (1994), " 'Most Cases Settle': Judicial Promotion and Regulation of Settlements," 46 *Stan. L. Rev.* 1339.]

Page 250. *Add the following sentence to the end of the paragraph under the heading "Court-Annexed Arbitration":*

See Lisa Bernstein (1993), "Understanding the Limits of Court-Connected ADR: A Critique of Federal Court-Annexed ADR Programs," 141 *U. Pa. L. Rev.* 2169.

Page 251. *Add the following sentence at the end of the paragraph above the heading "Summary Jury Trial":*

For a careful empirical study of early neutral evaluation in the U.S. District Court for the Northern District of California, see Joshua D. Rosenberg and H. Jay Folberg (1994), "Alternative Dispute Resolution: An Empirical Analysis," 46 *Stan. L. Rev.* 1487.

Page 271.   *At the top of the page, before the Questions, add*
           the following sentence to the end of the
           paragraph:

[For other analyses of the issues involved in mandatory ADR, see Lucy
Katz (1993), "Compulsory Alternative Dispute Resolution and Volunteerism: Two-Headed Monster or Two Sides of the Coin?" *J. Disp. Resol.* 1;
and Andreas Nelle (1992), "Making Mediation Mandatory: A Proposed
Framework," 7 *Ohio St. J. on Disp. Resol.* 287.]

Page 273.   *Add the following sentence to the end of the*
           paragraph at the bottom of the page:

[In accord with the *Strandell* case, see *In re NLO*, 5 F.3d 154 (6th Cir.
1993).]

Page 276.   *Add the following article before the Questions:*

E. SHERMAN, COURT-MANDATED ALTERNATIVE DISPUTE RESOLUTION: WHAT FORM OF PARTICIPATION SHOULD BE REQUIRED?

46 SMU L. Rev. 2079, 2089–2111 (1993)

A.   GOOD FAITH PARTICIPATION

Over the past several years some judges in ordering parties to participate in ADR proceedings have included a provision that they must
participate in good faith. A number of states have also adopted, by
statute or rule, a good faith participation requirement for mediation
or ADR. . . .

1.   INADEQUACY OF CASE PRECEDENTS FOR POLICY GUIDANCE

. . . The recent court-annexation of ADR processes has resulted in
few decisions in either federal or state courts concerning required
participation in ADR, and such decisions provide little policy guidance
as to what kind of participation is required. In most cases courts have
relied on Rule 16 (or an equivalent in state courts) or on inherent
judicial authority for their power to sanction for nonparticipation. The
decisions that have addressed the issue tend to rely on narrow questions

of a court's authority to make such an order or on the appropriateness of the sanctions imposed for noncompliance. . . .

Other cases have determined that the applicable statute did not, in fact, require "good faith participation.". . .

Some cases have simply found that the conduct did not amount to an absence of good faith. . . .

2.   INADEQUACY OF THE COLLECTIVE BARGAINING ANALOGY

A possible source for policy guidance in applying the "good faith participation" requirement is collective bargaining. Under the labor laws, unions and management that are required to engage in collective bargaining must bargain in good faith. Is that an apt analogy for ADR? Both ADR and collective bargaining would undoubtedly benefit from the parties' good faith participation. But there are differences in ADR which suggest that such participation is not as critical to the process as in collective bargaining and that the content of "good faith participation" is more difficult to determine. . . .

. . . Negotiators are not obligated to demonstrate an intent to find a basis for agreement, or to display a sincere desire to reach common ground, or to respond to and counter meaningfully the offers of the other side. ADR offers a process of assisted negotiation where the parties should be able to choose to be forthcoming and make concessions or not. To deny them the right to take strong, or even extreme, positions (for example, that there is no liability or that a certain sum is the only basis on which a settlement is possible) would deprive them of litigant autonomy and the legitimate right to hold out and have those issues determined in a trial. The level of accommodation to the other side required in collective bargaining is clearly unsuitable for ADR.

One further consideration operating against the use of the good faith participation standard in ADR is its inherent ambiguity. Phrased in terms of subjective intent, it seems to require an examination into a party's motives rather than its objective conduct. Its subjectivity raises the spectre of courts having to make complex investigations into the bargaining process of an ADR proceeding upon any party's claim of bad faith participation by another. The possibility of satellite litigation seeking sanctions for bad faith participation could severely undermine its claim to economy and efficiency.

Sanction motions also raise difficult issues of confidentiality. Many jurisdictions accord confidentiality to ADR. Proper determination of a sanction motion for bad faith participation could require the parties and the third party neutral to testify concerning communications made during the ADR proceeding. Courts would thus be faced with either rejecting confidentiality in bad faith participation cases (thereby undermining the need to encourage candor in ADR), or upholding confidentiality (thereby denying the parties access to crucial evidence on the participation issue). . . .

B.   EXCHANGE OF POSITION PAPERS AND OBJECTIVE INFORMATION

If a "good faith participation" requirement is undesirable in ADR, there are forms of participation that would enhance the likelihood of success that rely on objective conduct and therefore are more easily enforced by courts. For any form of ADR to succeed, there must be some indication of the parties' positions on the relevant issues and some exchange of basic factual information. Requiring the parties to provide each other and the third-party neutral with position papers and other relevant information lays a basis for meaningful consideration of the case without mandating specific forms of presentation or interaction with the other party. It encourages further oral participation and interaction without having to specify its form, since once having submitted a position paper, parties and counsel are less likely to refuse to discuss their positions at the ADR proceeding.

A reasonable order would be that the parties provide a position paper in advance of the ADR proceeding which would include a plain and concise statement of: (1) the legal and factual issues in dispute, (2) the party's position on those issues, (3) the relief sought (including a particularized itemization of all elements of damage claimed), and (4) any offers and counter-offers previously made. This is a shortened list of the kinds of items that are routinely required by federal courts in proposed pretrial orders under the authority of the Rule 16 pretrial conference rule.

The order might also require the parties to provide to the other side in advance, or to bring to the ADR proceeding, certain documents, such as current medical reports or specific business records. It would thus also serve as a discovery or subpoena order. . . .

C.   MINIMAL MEANINGFUL PARTICIPATION

Although exchange of position papers and objective information often provides an alternative to mandating a specific level of participation in ADR, there can still be a need for a minimal level of oral participation by the parties if the process is to have a genuine hope of success. It is not easy to fashion a term to describe what that minimal level should be because the necessary degree of participation varies with the type of ADR process involved. For want of a better term, I have adopted the language used by some courts that require the parties to participate "in a meaningful manner." Although hardly a model of certainty and precision, a "minimal meaningful participation" standard avoids the subjectivity of "good faith participation" by suggesting that the degree of participation required to be "meaningful" is related to the goal of the ADR procedure. Since the methodology and objectives of ADR processes vary a good deal, the "minimal meaningful participation" standard allows flexibility of participation depending on the particular process involved in each case.

1. MEANINGFUL PARTICIPATION VARIES WITH TYPE OF ADR

The distinction between "facilitative ADR," on the one hand, and "evaluative" or "trial run" ADR on the other, is useful for judging the degree of participation that is "meaningful" for achieving the ADR goals. "Facilitative ADR," such as mediation, is the least structured process and should require the least amount of formal participation. It is true that mediation works best when the parties interact on all levels, and it has been argued that "the client should be obliged respectfully to consider, and reconsider, with the other parties or the judicial host, the positions and the interests of both sides, and to think about ways to resolve the dispute." The trouble with this definition of the participation requirement is that it trenches deeply on litigant autonomy and, because of its subjectivity, would be difficult for a court to enforce. That is not to say that parties should not be encouraged to undertake such interactive participation as would be conducive to good mediation results, but that courts should not require it of them.

The objective of mediation is to get the parties to communicate in the broad interests of settlement, and thus mediation requires at least briefly indicating one's positions as to the relevant issues, listening to the other side, and reacting to the other side's positions. Unlike "evaluative" and "trial run" ADR processes, a comprehensive presentation of the case is not necessarily required. Assuming that there is no serious disparity between the parties as to opportunity to obtain information, they should be entitled to provide only that information that they choose to reveal. A failure to address or to disclose information as to all issues may suggest weakness to the other party and lower its willingness to make offers, but that is a strategic risk a party should be entitled to take. One objective of mediation is to identify the underlying interests of the parties in the hope of finding a solution that satisfies both sides. Nevertheless, as in any negotiation, disguising of true interests and bottom lines cannot be prohibited, for otherwise the courts would be enmeshed in judging subjective negotiation behavior that could severely abridge litigant autonomy.

The anti-coercion and litigation-autonomy policies underlying court-annexed ADR would also contravene any requirement of affirmative offer behavior, such as collective bargaining-type requirements that a party make an offer or counteroffer, avoid making predictably unacceptable offers or surface bargaining, or refrain from extreme demands or inflexible positions. A proper minimal meaningful participation requirement should be restricted to what is essential for the mediation process, that is, that the parties state their position(s) and listen to the other side's position(s). This might be described in short as a requirement that the parties must "discuss settlement," although no specific content, other than stating and reacting to positions, should be mandated. . . .

In contrast to mediation, "evaluative" forms of ADR require more participation from a party. For a proper evaluation by a third-party neutral in evaluative processes such as "early neutral evaluation" or "outcome determinative" or "evaluative" mediation, there must be a fairly comprehensive presentation of the issues of fact and law. An evaluation based on a sketchy or incomplete exploration of the case risks inaccuracy and unreliability by the evaluator. . . .

Similarly, in a "trial run" ADR proceeding, a good deal more is expected of the parties than just to talk, listen, and respond. Trial run processes contemplate a presentation of each side's case to various third parties so they can make a non-binding decision—to attorney or other expert arbitrators in court-annexed arbitration, to a jury in a summary jury trial, or to the parties' principal decision-makers in a mini-trial. For each of these processes to provide a reasonably accurate picture of how the case might play out if it went to trial, the parties are expected accurately to summarize their evidence and present their best arguments. These objectives may be jeopardized if the two sides do not provide a minimal level of formal presentation.

The one reported decision that has considered the participation requirement in a "trial run" ADR process is unsatisfactory in its analysis of the policy issues. In *Gilling v. Eastern Airlines, Inc.,* [680 F. Supp. 169 (D.N.J. 1988)] a suit by a passenger against an airline, the parties were ordered to participate in a court-annexed arbitration. The defense counsel presented only summaries of her position and read a few passages from deposition testimony and answers to interrogatories. When asked by the arbitrator at the end of the proceeding whether she wanted any damage award that he might make to be broken down into compensatory and punitive damages, she said "Do what you want, or, we don't care what you do, we won't pay it anyway." The arbitrator found that she merely "went through the motions," rendering the proceeding "a sham." In awarding sanctions, the court deferred to the arbitrator's judgment in weighing "the earnestness of the defendants' presentation against the gravity of the plaintiffs' allegations and the defendants' potentially sizeable exposure to liability" and to "his overall assessment of the meaningfulness of their participation."

The defense counsel's refusal to make any presentation as to damages would seem to violate a proper minimal meaningful participation requirement. Damages are central to a trial run form of ADR, and the arbitrator's evaluation could be severely crippled if a party refuses entirely to present its position or any information as to the damages issue. However, the imposition of sanctions because the defense counsel put on only summaries of her positions and read a few portions of depositions and interrogatories is troubling because it involves the court in judging just how much material must be presented. The arbitrator's finding that she merely "went through the motions" is a subjective commentary on the level of motivation behind her presentation. Litigant autonomy should allow counsel a fair degree of selective choice in what she presents. Unless the portions of depositions and interrogatories that she read were irrelevant or failed completely to address the issues in the case, the court should not have determined, on that basis alone, that she did not satisfy the participation standard. Even in a trial run process, a party or his attorney should be allowed to sift and choose what is to be presented without risk of sanction.

It appears that the arbitrator was especially angered by the fact that the defense counsel was contemptuous of the process. However, sanctions based on the attitude of the participant seem highly undesirable. There may be some point at which a party or counsel is so abusive of the other party or the neutral third-party, or so contemptuous in its behavior, that a court's sanction power should be invoked. It does not appear that that point was reached here. Any attempt to tightly monitor the quality and spirit of counsel's participation ultimately undercuts the values and objectives of court-mandated ADR and presents an unsatisfactory prospect of satellite litigation.

2.   REQUIRED PARTICIPATION SHOULD NOT INTERFERE WITH TRIAL STRATEGY

Consistency with the objectives of court-mandated ADR requires that a minimal meaningful participation standard not materially interfere with the parties' ultimate ability to present their cases to a jury. Two prominent cases have wrestled with situations where parties refused to comply with ADR orders because they feared that they would jeopardize their strategic position in a trial. These cases demonstrate that such claims are easily made and must be carefully scrutinized by courts. They also indicate that courts can sometimes take procedural steps that will allay a party's strategic concerns with participation. [Professor Sherman then discusses, inter alia, the *Strandell* case, casebook, p. 271 and concludes that the court's reliance on the plaintiff's right to protect a privileged work product was misplaced.]

D.   OBLIGATION TO ATTEND WITH SETTLEMENT AUTHORITY

Court orders that the parties participate in ADR proceedings often provide that they must attend with "full authority to settle the case" and, in the case of a corporate party or governmental body, that a representative attend who has authority to settle. Such orders raise questions, first, as to what persons are included when parties are ordered to attend, and, second, as to what kind of settlement authority the parties and/or attorneys must have.

1.   MANDATORY CLIENT ATTENDANCE

The conviction that it is essential for the parties to attend settlement proceedings has been relatively late in coming. . . .

Professor Riskin has made an examination of the advantages and disadvantages of client attendance that offers useful guidance for courts [see casebook, p. 445]. . . .

On balance, required attendance of individual parties at ADR proceedings is consistent with the four principles of court-mandated ADR. Client participation reduces coercion by providing full information to the person who must ultimately decide whether to settle and enhances litigant autonomy by allowing the client to participate in the presentation of his own case. It strengthens the feeling of the parties that they have had their day in court. Its compatibility with the ability of the ADR process to achieve its objectives varies with the process. It is certainly consistent with the objectives of "facilitative" ADR by including the client as an active participant in searching for solutions. It may not be as important in "evaluative" or "trial run" ADR, as the attorney usually plays the key role in summarizing and presenting the case, but the client can often add a critical aspect to both the case presentation and the negotiation that is expected to follow.

An exception to this analysis is when a named party has no real interest in the case. This frequently arises in personal-injury or property-damage cases filed against a fully insured defendant. Under standard insurance policy provisions, the insurance company has sole authority over the defense of cases, including whether to settle or go to trial. The insurance company representative, therefore, is the crucial person on the defense side for settlement negotiations. The insured defendant may have some interest in the case since its conduct is in question, but determination of that issue may have no monetary consequences to it. Most insured defendants are content to leave settlement matters to the insurance company, with no interest in devoting time and emotional capital to participating in settlement negotiations. An appropriate court order, therefore, would not require an insured defendant to attend when it has no realistic exposure over policy limits and when its consent to settle is not required. It is quite different, however, if there is any realistic possibility of recovery against the defendant above policy limits. . . .

Difficult questions also arise when the client is not an individual but a corporation. [Professor Sherman here discusses the *Heileman Brewing* case, casebook, p. 274.]

2. SCOPE OF SETTLEMENT AUTHORITY

Courts also routinely include in ADR orders a requirement that the parties and counsel come to the proceeding with settlement authority. This is based on the frequent experience that a settlement is less likely to be achieved if persons not in attendance must approve the settlement agreed upon. Coming without full settlement authority has also been seen as an illegitimate tactic used by parties, particularly insurance companies, to allow the negotiator to claim inability to bargain outside of a prescribed range and to allow absent officials to disavow agreements made by their negotiating representative as outside their authority. . . .

The hard cases arise when the representative's settlement authority is . . . ambiguous. . . . Assume that an insurance company sends a representative with authority to settle only up to $10,000, on the basis that it has thoroughly reviewed the case and is convinced that there is no liability at all and, that, in any event, the reasonable damages are much smaller than that amount. Surely the company should not be required to give its representative authority to settle at a higher amount when it has concluded that there is no justification for doing so. But the key inquiry is what the representative's instructions are. If he is sent without authority to consider any settlement above $10,000, this is essentially a "no authority" case. . . . A court should be entitled to require that the representative at least be open to hearing the arguments of the other side with the possibility of settling at any amount found to be persuasive, even though the representative understands that the company has evaluated the case as not worth more than $10,000. If his authority and instructions are so limited that he is deaf to any persuasion, then he is not the proper representative with adequate authority that the court has ordered.

A further question, however, is whether the representative must himself possess full authority to settle. Would it be sufficient to have a representative at the regional office with broader settlement authority be available by phone? What is troubling with this approach is that the person with the ultimate authority cannot be subjected to the discussion that takes place in the settlement conference, thus undermining the effectiveness of the process. On the other hand, requiring the representative to be the person with ultimate settlement authority can impose enormous burdens on that official's time or force her to delegate the authority further down the line than she finds it prudent to do.

G. Heileman Brewing Co., Inc. v. Joseph Oat Corp. wrestled with these issues. The majority upheld the magistrate's order that the defendant send a "corporate representative with authority to settle" on the ground that it did not require coming to court "willing to settle on someone else's terms," but only "to consider the possibility of settlement." . . .

Should a corporation (or a governmental body which can only act by the vote of a governing group) be required to rearrange its structure in order to give its negotiator full settlement authority? The answer would seem to depend on whether the authority-structure is reasonable (or required by law) and whether it can be accommodated by reasonable procedures to permit the negotiating representative to obtain ultimate approval. Normally, it would appear, a company should not be able to avoid sending a person with settlement authority just because it wants to limit that authority to someone higher up who cannot attend. It seems reasonable to expect the representative to be a person with suitable authority and discretion to engage in meaningful bargaining. . . .

How should a court treat governmental entities which are subject to internal regulations or statutory limitations that restrict settlement authority to high-level officials? In *In re Stone,* [986 F.2d 898 (5th Cir. 1993)] federal agencies and entities (including the Internal Revenue Service and Government National Mortgage Association) sought to mandamus a federal district judge from enforcing a standing order that required the federal government to send a representative with "full settlement authority" to settlement conferences. U.S. Attorneys may settle cases up to $500,000; if the client agency disagrees with the U.S. Attorney as to terms of settlement an Assistant Attorney General must approve the settlement; and settlements in classes of important cases must always be approved by the Deputy Attorney General or an Assistant Attorney General. The government argued that a court may never compel the Department of Justice to alter its settlement-authority regulations.

The Fifth Circuit disagreed, but cautioned that courts "must consider the unique position of the government as a litigant." It found that the purpose of the AG's regulations was to promote centralized decisionmaking on important questions; this serves the important objectives of allowing the government to act consistently, to pursue policy goals more effectively by placing authority in the hands of a few officials, and to promote political accountability. It concluded that, given these reasonable policy justifications and the insignificant interference with the operation of courts by respecting these regulations, the standing order was an abuse of discretion as applied in the particular cases involved.

The Fifth Circuit opinion went on to recommend that district courts take "a practical approach" to imposing settlement-authority requirements and consider "less drastic steps" before requiring the attendance of an official with ultimate settlement-authority. It suggested, for example, that a court could require the government to declare whether a case could be settled within the local U.S. Attorney's authority, and, if so, require him to attend or be available by telephone. A court could also take such actions as requiring the government to advise it who has settlement authority and then advising such person in advance of the conference to consider settlement and be fully prepared and available by telephone to discuss settlement at the time of the conference. Only if such lesser measures fail, should a court resort to requiring the attendance of the official with full settlement authority. . . .

Page 294.   Add the following sentence at the end of the last paragraph before the Questions:

For a recent study of the impact of private judging, see Elizabeth Rolph, Erik Moller, and Laura Peterson (1994), *Escaping the Courthouse: Private Alternative Dispute Resolution in Los Angeles* (Santa Monica: Rand Institute for Civil Justice).

Page 295.   Add to the References:

BERNSTEIN, Lisa (1993) "Understanding the Limits of Court-Connected ADR: A Critique of Federal Court-Annexed ADR Programs," 141 *U. Pa. L. Rev.* 2169.

CENTER FOR DISPUTE SETTLEMENT (1992) *National Standards for Court-Connected Mediation Programs*. Washington, D.C.: CDS.

GALANTER, Marc, and Mia CAHILL (1994) " 'Most Cases Settle': Judicial Promotion and Regulation of Settlements," 46 *Stan. L. Rev.* 1339.

KATZ, Lucy (1993) "Compulsory Alternative Dispute Resolution and Volunteerism: Two-Headed Monster or Two Sides of the Coin?" *J. Disp. Resol.* 1.

NELLE, Andreas (1992) "Making Mediation Mandatory: A Proposed Framework," 7 *Ohio St. J. on Disp. Resol.* 287.

PLAPINGER, Elizabeth, and Margaret SHAW (1992) *Court ADR: Elements for Program Design*. New York: Center for Public Resources Institute for Dispute Resolution.

RESNIK, Judith (1994) "Whose Judgment? Vacating Judgments, References for Settlement, and the Role of Adjudication at the Close of the Twentieth Century," 41 *U.C.L.A. L. Rev.* 1471.

RESNIK, Judith (1995) "Many Doors? Closing Doors? Alternative Dispute Resolution and Adjudication," 10 *Ohio J. on Disp. Resol.* 211.

ROLPH, Elizabeth, Erik MOLLER, and Laura PETERSON (1994) *Escaping the Courthouse: Private Alternative Dispute Resolution in Los Angeles*. Santa Monica: Rand Institute for Civil Justice.

SHERMAN, Edward (1993) "Court-Mandated Alternative Dispute Resolution: What Form of Participation Should be Required?" 46 *SMU L. Rev.* 2079.

Chapter 7
Family Disputes

Page 322.   *Add the following article before the Questions:*

J. PEARSON, FAMILY MEDIATION

**In National Symposium on Court-Connected Dispute Resolution
Research,** *A Report on Current Research Findings—Implications for Courts
and Future Research Needs* **51–77 (State Justice Institute, 1994)**

[Dr. Pearson, a sociologist, summarizes the results of 15 empirical studies of divorce mediation conducted by a variety of researchers over a 15-year period.]

Settlement Rates: There is little doubt that mediation is effective in disposing of a substantial proportion of contested custody and visitation cases for courts. Across studies, settlement rates stand in the 50–75 percent range. . . .

In addition to producing agreements during the sessions, several evaluations also find that mediation has various "spillover" effects that translate into more voluntary agreement-making and less judicial decision-making. . . .

Court Costs and Processing Times: Despite the impressive agreement rates produced in most divorce mediation programs, they appear to have little impact on the courts' overall workload. Contested custody and visitation cases comprise a small proportion of the domestic relations calendar. . . .

Another reason for the modest effects of mediation programs on court costs and workload is that many courts require that the parties appear in court before being referred to mediation and after mediation to present agreements to the court. . . .

Mediation programs may actually increase the number of post-divorce court appearances that occur in such cases. This was the conclusion reached by researchers at the NCSC who assessed samples of couples who mediated and used traditional court procedures in four different states and observed higher numbers of hearings among the mediation samples at some sites. They speculate that this is because mediators often sensitize parents to the need to revise visiting plans periodically to reflect the changing needs of children and as a result, mediating couples return to court to make periodic adjustments. . . . Evaluators of Washington D.C.'s Multi-Door Court House conclude that mediation increases resources expended by the court per case if mediator time and program administration costs are taken into account. . . .

Litigant Cost Savings: There is much less ambivalence in the research literature on the impact of mediation on savings to the parties in attorneys' fees. Virtually all studies that examine this issue find evidence of cost savings. . . .

User Satisfaction: Another strong area of consensus in the evaluation literature is the high level of user satisfaction with both the mediation process and the outcomes it generates. With few exceptions, study after study concludes that mediation is consistently favored as compared with adversarial interventions. Most assessments find that user satisfaction falls in the 70–90 percent range. These patterns do not differ for users of mandatory versus voluntary mediation programs, challenging the notion that mediation cannot be effective and liked unless participation is voluntary. . . .

Some common themes that run through many of the client satisfaction evaluations are an appreciation of the opportunity to express a point of view without interruption; the professionalism, control, and neutrality displayed by the mediator; the understandability of the process and the outcomes generated in it; and the opportunity to focus on the children and the issues pertaining to their care. . . .

Overall, the mediation research literature finds few differences in the reactions of men versus women to the mediation experience. Where gender differences appear, they tend to favor women. . . .

User Dissatisfaction: Not everyone reacts to mediation with enthusiasm: all evaluations reveal at least some level of client disaffection; a few evaluations reveal high incidences of disappointment. . . .

Types of Agreements: . . . While some studies find evidence of generosity in mediation agreements and others reveal the opposite, the general consensus across the studies is that agreements produced in different forums resemble one another in many important ways. Moreover, other legal changes, such as child support guidelines, have had the effect of reducing variation in divorce agreements.

Thus, while early evaluations revealed a tendency for mediating couples to opt for joint legal custody arrangements as compared with sole maternal custody arrangements in adversarial samples, more recent evaluations fail to find distinct custody outcomes among those who mediate. . . .

Assessments of property division and alimony awards in mediated and non-mediated agreements reveal that they are comparable and reflect prevailing legal norms, with wives receiving just over half the property and alimony being awarded about 20 to 25 percent of the time, mainly in lengthy marriages and high paternal income situations.

Finally, direct questioning about the incidence of custody blackmail in mediation reveals that it is a relatively rare phenomenon. . . .

Compliance and Relitigation: Although the evidence regarding the compliance and relitigation patterns associated with mediated and adjudicated agreements is somewhat mixed, several longitudinal studies find short-term improvements in compliance and relitigation for those who mediate. . . .

Given . . . contradictory findings, it may be safest to conclude that while mediation is not more effective than adjudication in promoting long-term compliance and preventing relitigation, mediated agreements are no more unstable than those originating from judicial forums or lawyer-conducted negotiations.

Relationships with Ex-Spouses and Adjustment of Children and Adults: Research results on spousal relationships and the psychological adjustment of children and adults following divorce underscore that mediation is a brief intervention that essentially produces short-term effects. While several studies find that mediation produces impressive short-term reductions in conflict and higher levels of cooperation among mediation participants, these advantages do not appear to last. . . .

Mandatory vs. Voluntary: As to mandatory approaches, several studies comparing mandatory mediation clients with their voluntary counterparts find that agreement rates are comparable as are satisfaction levels, willingness to recommend the process to others, and support for mandatory formats. . . .

Mediator Characteristics and Training: . . . Comparisons of lawyer-trained versus social worker-trained mediators in the [Denver Custody Mediation Project] also failed to reveal consistent differences. Indeed, the only background characteristic that was associated with more favorable outcomes was the experience level of the mediator. For both lawyers and social workers, agreement rates and approval ratings improved significantly after they had mediated five cases. A recent evaluation of mandatory, comprehensive mediation in Maine finds support for the use of volunteer lay people who present little threat to the role of lawyers in the divorce process. . . .

*Page 325.   Add the following article and text before the
            Lerman mediation article:*

C.   MCEWEN AND N. ROGERS, BRING THE
LAWYERS INTO DIVORCE MEDIATION

Disp. Resol. Mag. 8–10 (Summer 1994)*

Critics of divorce mediation paint a picture of divorcing parties who
enter mediation with bargaining imbalances and encounter a mediator
who exacerbates the inequality. The solution, according to prominent
critics such as Professors Trina Grillo and Penelope Bryant, is to let the
parties choose whether to participate in mediation. In other words, to
preserve fairness in divorce mediation, critics advocate eliminating the
mandatory mediation programs now operating in about ten percent of
the nation's domestic relations courts.

Those supporting mandatory mediation either do not accept the
unfairness charges or, taking a middle ground, contend that mandatory
mediation can be regulated to assure that any bargaining imbalances
are redressed. This middle-ground approach has produced considerable
regulation: a few statutory provisions directed toward preserving fairness in 34 states and a substantial number of provisions in 17 states.
For example, without any evidence of their effectiveness in safeguarding
fairness, legislatures have variously imposed duties on mediators to
assure fairness, required case-by-case selection to eliminate cases with
predictable bargaining imbalances, limited issues covered by the mediation to custody and visitation, and set up strict mediator qualifications
including requirements for advanced academic degrees. Not only does
it seem unlikely that these recent statutes will promote fairness, but they
also threaten to undermine one of mediation's defining advantages:
spontaneity and flexibility in responding to the parties' needs and
circumstances.

There is another possible solution to fairness concerns in divorce
mediation: encourage the parties to bring their lawyers to the mediation
session. Commentators rarely discuss this option, however, because of
their assumptions about divorce mediation and attorneys. In essence,
all sides in the debate about fairness in divorce mediation imagine
lawyers who are strenuous advocates in court but absent from mediation
because they would "spoil" the process by their domineering and aggressive approach. Further, they assume that divorcing parties will re-

*See also MCEWEN, Craig A., Nancy H. ROGERS, and Richard J. MAIMAN (1995)
"Bring in the Lawyers: Challenging the Dominant Approaches to Ensuring Fairness in
Divorce Mediation," 79 *Minn. L. Rev.* 601.

solve their cases in court if not in mediation. Although these assumptions may be correct some of the time, they are not always so. Take Maine's experience, for example.

Since 1984, Maine has mandated mediation in contested divorce cases involving minor children. Mediation is not confined to questions of custody and visitation, but may include financial matters as well. Maine lawyers have counseled thousands of clients going through this mandatory process. The results of interviews with 88 Maine divorce lawyers lead us to believe that mandatory mediation can be fair if it includes all divorce-related issues, and if lawyers are encouraged to participate with their clients. The interviews also reveal that the assumptions leading mediation proponents and critics to ignore our approach are in fact myths.

The *first myth* that critics and advocates of mandatory mediation share is that lawyers disappear when mediation begins. For advocates the disappearance of lawyers is often a goal because presumably it diminishes adversary conduct, empowers parties, and reduces costs. For critics it is a central problem because lawyers are seen as guardians of client rights, and their absence disadvantages weaker parties especially.

In Maine, however, divorce lawyers do not vanish when mediation starts. Indeed, 95 percent of those attorneys interviewed reported that they always or usually attend mediation sessions with their clients. Not only do lawyers attend, but they participate actively, though selectively, on behalf of their clients. Their presence and participation are premised on concerns about fairness because they recognize, as one lawyer said, that "mediation is like a crucible and bad decisions can be made." That is, even the best and most balanced mediation can create a momentum toward settlement that may lead parties to disregard their interests. But lawyers are also concerned about unfairness resulting from pressures from the other party and from the mediator. One lawyer reflected a common view among those interviewed: "I'm there to protect [my client] if I think things are not being run fairly and to watch out for his or her interests, but primarily it's up to him or her, the mediator, and the other spouse." Lawyers also recognize that some clients may need support in articulating their interests and concerns if fair results are to be achieved. As one lawyer said, "It depends on the client, but I'll tell them, 'If you want to talk, feel free to talk. The mediator would rather have you talk, but if you prefer me to talk, that's fine.' "

Thus, unlike the common picture of a lawyerless process, Maine divorce mediation involves lawyers actively, and they participate with an eye toward fairness.

A *second myth* about divorce mediation is that lawyer participation would spoil the mediation process for parties by permitting attorneys to take over the process. Further, it is supposed, lawyers will argue the law and pursue aggressive adversarial tactics in mediation, ruining efforts at settlement. This view is shared by many advocates of mediation and has produced statutes or court rules in five states prohibiting lawyer participation in custody mediation altogether or limiting the attorney role to observer. Opponents of mandatory mediation, on the other hand, assume that lawyers, by providing the vigorous advocacy necessary to assert and protect client rights, would thwart a mediation process that "steamrolls" the parties.

The view of lawyers as habitual spoilers proves erroneous in Maine. That state reports settlement rates of about 50 percent in its fairly short, single-session mediations, a figure comparable to those in many other divorce mediation programs where lawyers do not participate. Settlements even with lawyers present seem to happen because the mediator's demeanor and the mediation setting encourage lawyers to behave in accord with the professional norm of the "reasonable lawyer," who discourages unrealistic client expectations, refrains from identifying with the client emotionally, resists inflating demands, understands the likely legal outcome, and engages straightforwardly in the settlement process. In fact, lawyers sometimes report that the usual structure of mediation sessions discourages antagonistic conduct by lawyers: "It's easy to be Tarzan over the telephone, it really is. It's real hard to pull that garbage when the client [is right there]."

Even with their lawyers present, clients participate because that is the expectation of the mediator. Thus, one lawyer's description of her relationship to her client in mediation was typical of Maine lawyers: "I want to sit back and listen, and I'm not going to interrupt unless I feel that you've misstated something or you're misinformed on an area or need some counseling."

This client involvement allows parties to voice their feelings and to identify and deal with intensely important emotional issues that may block settlement. Said one lawyer: "I'm much more inclined to let the client talk in the mediation room. . . . [I]t's one of the few times [the parties] have the opportunity to be face-to-face, and they need to get some stuff off their chest, and it can be done in that setting safely and usefully." The chance for parties to talk is prized and encouraged by most lawyers. "This is the only opportunity I have," said another lawyer, "to have [the other spouse] sitting there listening to my client's point of view. He's probably never done it before in his life. Now he's got someone who's describing what her life is going to be like, going through her budget."

Parties in Maine engage actively in most mediation sessions, express their feelings, and participate in settlement discussions. Their chances of achieving a fair result are increased both by the support of legal counsel and by their opportunity to take a leading role in crafting a divorce settlement for themselves.

The *third myth* about mandatory mediation is that it supplants trial. For mediation advocates this is its advantage because it gives the parties rather than a judge control over process and outcomes. For mediation critics this is mediation's weakness because it substitutes an informal process for one that presumably protects the rights of parties, especially weaker parties. But both advocates and critics are mistaken; most often mandated divorce mediation replaces or supplements *negotiation* rather than substitutes for trials. Trials, even in initially contested divorces, are relatively uncommon. Our research in Maine confirms that where mediation is mandated in contested cases, most parties who enter the process would have settled on their own in any event. However, mediation moves settlement to an earlier point.

Maine lawyers appreciate the advantages of mediation because it facilitates communication with clients and makes the negotiation process more efficient. By participating in mediation, lawyers can work more effectively with clients whose demands are perceived as unreasonable. As one lawyer pointed out: "Sometimes the mediator . . . will help me in my role with a client, if I have a hard sell with my client." That can happen because mediators can help "reality test" with parties in ways that lawyers find hard to do. Lawyers understandably worry about being too blunt in challenging their clients' demands and expectations, for fear of undermining the clients' confidence in them as resolute advocates. Mediation can help lawyers in such circumstances, as noted by most Maine lawyers. One lawyer said, for example, "At mediation, it's an opportunity for my client to kind of expose his or her case to reality, and the mediator many times is going to say, 'Wait, is that what you really mean?' " According to another attorney, "You can say, 'You can't get that.' You go to mediation, the mediation takes place and this and that, and it shows that it's not only my ideas. Then I can come out and say, 'Well I told you.' [Mediation] gives them almost a second opinion."

With such openings provided by a mediation process in which they participate, attorneys can more effectively advise clients about reasonable expectations for their divorces.

Lawyers also find that they can reduce some of the delay, cost, and frustration of negotiation by phone, letter, and fax—what one lawyer described as "months of diddling back and forth between lawyers." Instead, as another Maine lawyer described the mediation process, "Everybody's there. You don't have to say, 'Well, I've got to ask my client.'

If there's any confusion, they're both there to talk about it." Not only is this four-way meeting more efficient, it also reduces confusion and miscommunication, as may happen in the negotiation process when client tells lawyer who summarizes for the other lawyer who then translates for her client. "It gets them face-to-face with the other side," one lawyer said. "It eliminates all the rumors. [Often] clients tell me what their spouse said their lawyer said. All that smoke is gone when we sit down in mediation."

Mediation also introduces each attorney to the other party, so that they can see with their own eyes and hear with their own ears what he or she is like. With that better understanding negotiation can be more effective because a good attorney can better gauge the other parties' interests and needs.

The *final myth* is that all mediation is alike, either like the ideal mediation program the advocate envisions or the problematic one the critic abhors. Instead, as the Maine experience suggests and a wider comparison of mediation programs would show, mediation differs substantially from jurisdiction to jurisdiction. This variation provides the opportunity to assess various approaches in order to maximize the likelihood of fairness in mediation, while preserving its other values such as flexibility and low cost.

With these myths aside, we can entertain another approach to assuring fairness: including the lawyers as active participants in mandatory divorce mediation sessions. To do so would require repeal of the statutes proscribing such participation in a few jurisdictions. Lawyer participation is more likely, the Maine research indicates, if mandatory mediation extends to the economic issues that divorce attorneys view as strategically important. Broadening the issues covered by mediation would also necessitate statutory amendment in some states.

Certainly, we need to know more before advocating that divorce mediation everywhere be broadened to include economic issues and to encourage active participation by the parties' lawyers in the give and take of mediation sessions. However, our research into the effectiveness of the Maine approach leads us to think that the lawyered approach is superior, for several reasons:

- Statutes regulating divorce mediation provide little hope that fairness problems are eased by regulation;
- Regulation in other fields tends to be costly, and early analysis indicates that mediation is no exception;
- Adding lawyers to the mediation process may not increase the cost; with all parties present the efficiency of negotiation can be improved, it takes fewer sessions to complete mediation, additional

issues can be included, and mediators need not be as expert and, thus, as expensive.

In short, the critics of mandatory divorce mediation may be on target with their concerns about fairness, but are taking too narrow a view of possible solutions. By looking beyond the rhetoric and examining evidence of the operation of divorce mediation that includes lawyers, we can see new possibilities for resolving the fairness issue in divorce mediation. The alternatives to examining this fresh approach are to limit mediation to circumstances in which the parties agree to the mediation, to wink at unfairness, or to risk a heavily regulated mandatory mediation that will be less fair than the traditional system yet equally rigid and bureaucratic.

For a warning that lawyers may not negotiate effectively during mediation, see Bryan (1994). Would it help to train lawyers to represent clients effectively in mediation, in the ways suggested by Michael Lewis (Supplement, p. 27)?

Page 332.   Add to the References:

BRYAN, Penelope E. (1992) "Killing Us Softly: Divorce Mediation and the Politics of Power," 40 *Buff. L. Rev.* 441.

BRYAN, Penelope E. (1994) "Reclaiming Professionalism: The Lawyer's Role in Divorce Mediation," 28 *Fam. L.Q.* 177.

BUSH, Robert A. Baruch (1992) *The Dilemmas of Mediation Practice.* Washington, D.C.: National Institute for Dispute Resolution.

FISCHER, Karla, Neil VIDMAR, and Rene ELLIS (1993) "The Culture of Battering and the Role of Mediation in Domestic Violence Cases," 46 *SMU L. Rev.* 2117.

FRIEDMAN, Gary (1993) *A Guide to Divorce Mediation.* New York: Workman.

GAGNON, Andre G. (1992) "Ending Mandatory Divorce Mediation for Battered Women," 15 *Harv. Women's L.J.* 272.

HAYNES, John M. (1994) *The Fundamentals of Family Mediation.* Albany: State University of New York.

MCEWEN, Craig A., and Nancy H. ROGERS (1994) "Bring the Lawyers into Divorce Mediation," *Disp. Resol. Mag.* 8–10 (Summer).

MCEWEN, Craig A., Richard MAIMAN, and Lynn MATHER (1994) "Lawyers, Mediation, and the Management of Divorce Practice," 28 *L. & Soc'y Rev.* 249.

PORTLAND MEDIATION SERVICE (1992) *Mediation in Cases of Domestic Abuse:*

Helpful Option or Unacceptable Risks? The Final Report of the Domestic Abuse and Mediation Project. Portland, Me.: Portland Mediation Service.

ROSENBERG, Joshua (1991) "In Defense of Mediation," 33 *Ariz. L. Rev.* 467.

TREUTHART, Mary Pat (1993) "In Harm's Way? Family Mediation and the Role of the Attorney Advocate," 32 *Golden Gate U.L. Rev.* 717.

Chapter 8
Public Disputes

Page 356. After Question 8.9, add Question 8.10:

8.10 In early 1994, the Federal Communications Commission (FCC) convened a negotiated rulemaking committee for the purpose of negotiating rules relating to mobile telephone satellite services. The procedures used by the FCC in this negotiated rulemaking were described by one participant (Goldberg, 1994) as follows:

> The agency selected participants to represent all interests affected by the proposed rules, convened representatives of those interests to serve as a negotiated rulemaking advisory committee, and nominated a facilitator for the committee. The facilitator had technical expertise on the issues under consideration, as well as experience in chairing committees, but no dispute resolution experience as mediator or arbitrator.
>
> Most of the industry participants were represented by a team of lawyers and technical experts. The agency was represented by a senior technical expert, who was assisted by agency attorneys and members of the agency technical staff. All the industry participants believed that if no consensus was reached on proposed rules, the agency representative would play a significant role in the agency's internal deliberations regarding proposed rules. The agency representative was not, however, authorized to communicate the agency's views on the merits of the proposals made by industry representatives or the agency's likely action in the event no consensus was reached. Accordingly, he did not do so.

The negotiated rulemaking committee reached consensus on some issues, but did not do so on the central issue—a rule regarding the sharing of available spectrum by providers of mobile satellite services. Which, if any, aspects of the procedures used in the rulemaking may have contributed to the failure to reach consensus?

Page 357. Add the following to the References:

GOLDBERG, Stephen B. (1994) "Reflections on Negotiated Rulemaking," 9
Wash. Law. 42 (Sept./Oct.).

Chapter 9
International Disputes

Page 401.   Add the following to the References:

BERCOVITCH, Jacob, and Jeffrey RUBIN (1992) *Mediation in International Practice*. New York: St. Martin's.

FAURE, Guy, and Jeffrey RUBIN (1993) *Culture and Negotiation*. Newbury Park, Cal.: Sage.

PRINCEN, Thomas (1992) *Intermediaries in International Conflict*. Princeton: Princeton University Press.

RUBIN, Jeffrey, and Jeswald SALACUSE (1993) "International Negotiation," *Alternatives* 95 (July).

Chapter 10
Dispute Systems Design

Page 411.   Add the following text and Note after the first full paragraph and breaker line:

Examples of the practical application of dispute systems design principles have multiplied in recent years. Some of these are set out below.

Note: Managing conflict: The strategy of dispute systems design*

SIX PRINCIPLES OF DISPUTE SYSTEMS DESIGN

PRINCIPLE 1: PREVENTION

Subsequent to the publication of *Getting Disputes Resolved: Designing Systems to Cut the Costs of Conflict,* we have expanded the first principle of dispute systems design from "build in consultation before, feedback after" to "prevention." We have done so because we recognize that preventing disputes is part of the dispute systems designer's function, and that consultation and feedback are only two of many possible means to prevent disputes.

Another important means of preventing disputes is to deal with the behavior that is producing disputes. This is the approach that the U.S. Navy and Marine Corps have adopted in designing a system to deal with sexual harassment disputes. A central element in that system is sensitizing people to recognize potentially objectionable conduct. To do so, the Navy and Marine Corps adopted a simple but powerful metaphor: the stoplight. "Red" behavior is unacceptable; "yellow" is

---

*Except as hereafter indicated, this Note has been adapted from Brett, Goldberg, and Ury (1994).

potentially so; "green" is appropriate and encouraged. Examples are given of each to provide guidance in deterring conduct that might be construed as sexual harassment.

PRINCIPLE 2: PUT THE FOCUS ON INTERESTS

Putting the focus on interests is the central tenet of dispute systems design. Effective dispute resolution systems make full use of procedures that can help disputing parties seek an interests-based solution.

Mediation is a valuable means to ensure that interests are thoroughly considered before a dispute turns into a lawsuit. According to Motorola General Counsel Richard Weise, "Motorola has found mediation to be successful practically every time it's been used. . . . "If we can get them into mediation, we are confident that we can find a settlement. The difficulty is getting the other party to agree to mediate."

To use another example, the Southwest Texas Methodist Hospital dispute system includes a mediation clause as a condition of admission. When patients sign into the hospital, they agree to mediate any disputes with the hospital. Should a dispute arise, the agreement offers a face-saving way for both hospital and patient to enter into interests-based dispute resolution.

Brown & Root, a nationwide construction and engineering firm, has established a system for employee disputes that provides multiple opportunities for mediation. To make the process easily accessible, Brown & Root trained employees in interests-based mediation skills and made them available to mediate disputes between other employees and supervisors. While they have no authority over either, they know how to keep negotiations focused on interests. Mediation is also available from "advisors" who serve as ombudsmen for Brown & Root, as well as from many managers who have been trained in mediation skills. The dispute system also provides for mediation by outside neutrals selected through the American Arbitration Association.

PRINCIPLE 3: BUILD IN "LOOP-BACKS" TO NEGOTIATION

"Loop-backs" to negotiation are procedures that provide the parties with information about their rights or power and encourage them to reopen negotiations on the basis of that information. Information about how rights standards have been applied in other disputes can serve to narrow the gap between the parties' expectations of the outcomes of a rights contest and thus make agreement possible.

The claims resolution facilities that have been established in mass tort situations provide an interesting example of a "loop-back." When A.H. Robins, the manufacturer of the Dalkon Shield contraceptive device, sought bankruptcy protection in 1985, it asked the court to create a "closed fund" from which all present and future claimants would receive payments. The judge hired an expert to determine Robins' probable liability, and to develop a mechanism—the claims facility—for disbursing the monies reserved to cover that liability.

The expert and his team established an extensive data base including the 9,000 claims against Robins that had been resolved prior to 1985, and a sampling of the 300,000 cases that were filed subsequently in response to the court's advertising for claims. They developed full medical records for each case in the sample, as well as payment data for settled cases. Using the data from the settled cases, the team developed statistical weights that linked type and severity of medical condition with amount of payment. They then applied these weights to the unsettled cases and estimated Robins' total liability.

The analysis by the claims facility established a schedule of payments for various medical conditions potentially stemming from use of the Dalkon Shield. The claimant is offered statistical information about what he or she would likely receive in a court proceeding. This information can be used to help the parties "loop-back" to negotiations which take into account the unique particulars of the claim.

Experience with the Dalkon Shield and other claims facilities has demonstrated that such a facility needs to provide more than loop-back information about average outcomes to facilitate the resolution of claims. Claimants' willingness to accept facility-generated awards depends on whether or not they feel their circumstances have been considered. Thus, loop-back information is best accompanied by a procedure like mediation that focuses on the interests of the claimant in receiving as much compensation as possible and the interests of the claims facility in equitably distributing its limited assets.

PRINCIPLE 4: PROVIDE LOW-COST RIGHTS AND POWER PROCEDURES

A low-cost, rights-based dispute resolution system grew out of negotiations in the summer and fall of 1990 between creditors of Drexel, Burnham, Lambert (then in bankruptcy); securities fraud claimants against Drexel, whose claims totaled over $25 billion; and the U.S. Securities and Exchange Commission (SEC). The outcome of those negotiations was an agreement to divide Drexel's assets into two parts.

One part would go to creditors, and the other part, which ultimately totaled $228 million, would go to securities fraud claimants.

There was also a provision for $15 million to go to the securities fraud claimants to defray the expenses of allocating their portion of the settlement among them. Any unused portion of the $15 million was to be divided among the securities fraud claimants. These claimants, then, had a strong interest in an allocation process that would be fair, inexpensive, and speedy.

Allocating the available funds among the securities fraud claimants in a fair, inexpensive, and speedy manner presented a formidable challenge. There were over 200 claims, some of which were highly complex class claims, brought on behalf of hundreds of small investors; other claims were equally complex actions brought by banks, insurance companies, and other major corporations. Court proceedings, in which lawyers representing each claimant argued the merits of their claim, would likely have consumed a substantial portion of the claimant's recoveries. A creative solution was needed, and with the prompting of the SEC, which selected two dispute systems designers to advise it, a low-cost, rights-based dispute resolution system was designed.

This procedure, which was called the Subclass B Plan of Allocation, provided for the claimants to select a five-person Executive Committee from among the lawyers representing them. The SEC also appointed a representative to the Executive Committee—one of the dispute systems designers.

The Subclass B Plan of Allocation called for the Executive Committee to seek negotiated agreements with all claimants. In the event that negotiations were unsuccessful, the SEC representative was available to mediate. Any claims that could not be consensually resolved were to be assigned a value by the Executive Committee. The value of the unsettled claims as well as the value of those that were negotiated were to be presented to the district court for approval. The district court was authorized to submit unresolved claims to a special master for a recommended decision and then to the district court for final decision, or to proceed directly to a district court final decision.

In dispute systems design terms the Subclass B Plan of Allocation provided for negotiations (between the Executive Committee and claimants), mediation (by the SEC representative), an advisory decision (by a special master), and a final and binding decision by the district court. At each step, the focus was on rights (the legal merits of the claim).

In order to achieve fairness, the Subclass B Plan of Allocation provided that the Executive Committee would adopt guidelines for the uniform valuation of claims, and bar any Executive Committee member from participating in the resolution of any claim in which he had a financial interest. The SEC representative was charged with the responsibility of scrutinizing the overall fairness of the proceedings and the consistent application of the claims evaluation guidelines.

Increased speed and reduced costs were also achieved by using a special procedure for dealing with "small" claims—those under $100,000. Recognizing that the administrative costs of evaluating such claims might in many instances be greater than their value, and that all claimants had a financial interest in keeping administrative costs to a minimum, the Executive Committee decided that, without examining the merits of claims under $100,000, it would offer claimants 20 percent of the face amount of such claims. Claimants whose claims were greater than $100,000 were given the opportunity to reduce their claims to that amount and receive $20,000. In total, 23 claimants accepted small claims treatment for their claims.

Ultimately, the Subclass B Executive Committee entered into consensual agreements with all but one claimant. On August 18, 1994, U.S. District Court Judge Milton Pollack approved the agreements and denied the claim of the sole objector. The objector's appeal was denied, so that a low-cost rights-based dispute resolution system came to a successful end.

While the system developed to deal with the Drexel, Burnham, Lambert securities fraud claims was set up many years after the events giving rise to those claims, some low-cost rights-based systems achieve impressive results because they resolve disputes immediately. The need for high-speed dispute resolution has long been recognized in the construction industry, where many contractors work on the same project, and a dispute involving any of those contractors can interfere with the ability of others to continue working.

One means of providing high-speed dispute resolution is the dispute review board.* Such a board is typically composed of neutral industry experts, jointly selected by the owner(s) and the general contractor at the beginning of a construction project. The dispute review board meets periodically with the parties to preempt disputes and to promptly evaluate disputes if they occur. The board produces written recommendations, which are based on relevant contract provisions, applicable laws and regulations, and the facts of the dispute. While the recommendations of the board are intended to carry great weight for both the owner and the contractor, they are not binding on either party. They are, however, typically admissible as evidence in any subsequent dispute resolution proceeding.

---

*The following discussion of dispute review boards is drawn from Sander and Thorne (forthcoming 1995).

Since the first dispute review board was implemented in 1976 for the Second Bore of the Eisenhower Tunnel project in Colorado, the mechanism has been established in over 100 projects, totaling approximately $6.5 billion in construction. On these projects, over 100 disputes were referred to the review boards, and none have led to arbitration or litigation.

PRINCIPLE 5: ARRANGE PROCEDURES IN A LOW-TO-HIGH COST
SEQUENCE

The Federal Deposit Insurance Corporation uses a negotiation-mediation-arbitration ladder in its system for resolving disputes involving controlled entities such as receiverships. Dispute resolution coordinators in regional offices encourage their colleagues to negotiate the resolution of disputes. Disputes that are not resolved can be mediated at two different levels in the organization. Arbitration is reserved for the few disputes that are not resolved. In 1992 and 1993 only two of the more than 300 cases processed through its in-house system went to arbitration.

The state of Florida recently directed its 11 regional planning councils to develop a system for resolving growth management and planning disputes among local governments, regional agencies, and private interests. The regions agreed to a system consisting of four optional steps to be taken prior to commencing litigation: 1) situational assessment by the regional planning council or another neutral; 2) settlement meetings; 3) mediation; and 4) advisory decision-making. The intent is to use the system like a ladder, resolving as many disputes as possible through situation assessments and settlement meetings. The steps are not mandatory, however, and may be used in any sequence that appears to be appropriate for the dispute.

PRINCIPLE 6: PROVIDE THE NECESSARY TRAINING, RESOURCES,
INCENTIVES, AND ENVIRONMENT

This principle has been expanded since the publication of *Getting Disputes Resolved* to include "environment," in recognition that even the most carefully designed dispute resolution system may fail in an environment that is hostile to its goals. The greatest challenge to the Navy and Marine Corps dispute system for sexual harassment is a culture that did not find objectionable incidents such as those that occurred at the 1991 Tailhook convention. Recognizing this, the Navy and Marine

Corps have built their program on one of their core values, individual accountability, and have adopted the slogan "You are individually accountable. Do not ignore sexual harassment." They have also taken aggressive action to publicize the program and educate personnel. Early retirement of officers involved in or responsible for the Tailhook incident has demonstrated the commitment to change at the highest level. It is thus possible that the environment exists for the prevention and successful resolution of sexual harassment claims.

Motorola's first step in introducing systems design into its corporate law department was to frame the program in terms consistent with Motorola's strategy of "cycle-time reduction." Anticipating resistance to ADR from attorneys who were litigators, the design team stated the program's goal as reducing the "cycle-time" for the resolution of disputes by reducing dependence on litigation. The second step was to have Motorola's CEO sign the CPR Institute for Dispute Resolution ADR pledge (see casebook, p. 427) and sell the idea of the pledge to the attorneys in the law department. Richard Weise, Motorola's General Counsel, says of the pledge, "Read it. It does not say that you or your client are sissies. It acknowledges that you are practical cycle-time reducers, who can be approached without worrying that the other guy is giving signs of weakness." By tying its dispute resolution system to the corporate environment, Motorola is maximizing its potential for success.

Page 419. Add the following to the References:

BRETT, Jeanne M., Stephen B. GOLDBERG, and William L. URY (1994) "Managing Conflict: The Strategy of Dispute Systems Design," 6 Bus. Wk. Executive Briefing Service.

SANDER, Frank E. A., and Christopher M. THORNE (forthcoming 1995) "Dispute Resolution in the Construction Industry: The Role of Dispute Review Boards," — Construction L. Rep. 2d — .

SLAIKEU, Karl, and Ralph HASSON (1992) "Not Necessarily Mediation: The Use of Convening Clauses in Dispute Systems Design," 8 Neg. J. 331.

Chapter 11

Institutionalization

Page 427. *At the bottom of the page, add the following sentence to the end of the last paragraph:*

See *Alternatives,* May 1994, p. 66, for CPR Model ADR clauses.

Page 435. *Replace the discussion under Taxonomy, pp. 435–437, with the following article:*

F. SANDER AND S. GOLDBERG, FITTING THE FORUM TO THE FUSS: A USER-FRIENDLY GUIDE TO SELECTING AN ADR PROCEDURE
10 Neg. J. 49 (1994)

Mary Stone has worked for the past two years as an accounting manager at the Smith Corporation, a manufacturer of menswear. She is one of only two women in the Accounting Department.

Stone is an attractive single woman of 32. The fact that she is somewhat overweight has made her the object of various jokes around the office, some of them of an explicit sexual nature. Sometimes she will find a crude cartoon on her desk when she arrives in the morning (e.g., a recent one depicted a couple in bed, with the caption "Fat girls are best."); at other times she hears whispered comments about her as she passes by. Although this objectionable behavior has been going on for about four months, it has really got to Stone recently. Last week, she discussed the situation with the director of the Department of Human Resources, who urged her to see the sexual harassment counselor, Jane Willard. Willard promised to send around to the accounting department a reminder about the company's policies on sexual harassment.

Stone has now come to see you, an attorney who specializes in sexual harassment cases. Mindful of the recent emphasis on various ways of resolving disputes outside the courts, you wonder whether this case might be suitable for alternative dispute resolution (ADR).

What sort of questions should be considered in making this determination? [In the casebook text replaced by this article] we . . . identified such factors as the nature of the case, the relationship between the parties, the relief sought by the plaintiff, and the size and complexity of the claim. We suggested, for example, that if a dispute involves a run-of-the-mill tort claim that raises no novel legal questions, then some simple form of adjudication, such as arbitration, might be used, but that a novel claim raising significant legal questions that need judicial elaboration should go to court. Similarly, if the disputants have an ongoing relationship that has broken down, then mediation may be strongly indicated because of its capacity to deal with that issue.

That analysis, which was implicitly from a public policy perspective, considered which procedure would be best for *all* those with an interest in the dispute, not which procedure would be preferred by each individual disputant. In this article, we examine the suitability of various dispute resolution processes from the perspective of the parties to the dispute, and then from the public-interest perspective. We use this two-step approach because we believe that doing so provides a more realistic view of the manner in which decisions regarding the choice of dispute resolution procedure are made.

The initial determination regarding the choice of dispute resolution procedure will be made by each attorney in consultation with his or her client. In these consultations, both court and various types of ADR will, and perhaps must, be considered. Next, the attorneys will discuss with each other the decision each has reached with the client, and will seek to agree upon a procedure. If they do not agree, the complaining party will be free to take the dispute to court. Then, if the court has an ADR program, as is increasingly common, court personnel will decide if the dispute is suitable for some aspect of that program. If the court's ADR program is optional, the parties will be free to reject the court's recommendation; if that program is mandatory, the court will order the parties into some type of ADR.

As counsel for the disputing parties consider which dispute resolution procedure is appropriate for their clients, they face two basic questions: First, what are the client's goals, and what dispute resolution procedure is most likely to achieve those goals? Second, if the client is amenable to settlement, what are the impediments to settlement, and what ADR procedure is most likely to overcome those impediments?

When the decision regarding an appropriate dispute resolution procedure is made from a public perspective, the second question is similar to the kind of analysis an attorney should give to any client; the first question, however, is more complex. Initially, court personnel or public agencies making a recommendation regarding appropriate procedures for resolving a dispute must consider the goals of all parties to the dispute. Furthermore, they must consider the public interest in that dispute. While a private settlement may serve the interests of all parties to the dispute, the public interest may lie in public adjudication (e.g., because of a need for judicial interpretation of a newly enacted statute). . . .

CLIENT GOALS

In the hypothetical case with which we began this article, how do you, as Stone's attorney, prepare for your initial interview with your client? Is she eager to remain at the company (perhaps because alternative employment opportunities are scarce) and hence wants to resolve this situation with the least disruption and fuss? Or is she so angry that she is determined to have some outside neutral pronounce her "right," and thus vindicate her position?

Answers to questions like these are critical in determining what dispute resolution procedure is appropriate in this case. The fact that Stone has decided to come to an attorney indicates that she is dissatisfied with the present posture of the dispute. But should she file a lawsuit or seek some other way of resolving the problem? If she has an emotional need for vindication, she will have to resort to some form of adjudication, either in court or—if the company is willing—through private means, such as arbitration or private judging. . . . If Stone wants public vindication, however, or a binding precedent, only court will do.

A form of third-party vindication is available through the minitrial, the summary jury trial, and early neutral evaluation, since in each of these processes a neutral third party evaluates the contentions of the parties. Because these processes are both abbreviated and nonbinding, however, they will not always satisfy a client's desire for vindication.

If Stone wants the opinion of a neutral concerning the merits of her claim less for vindication than as a means of convincing the company that she has a strong claim, and is entitled to a reasonable settlement, then any of the nonbinding evaluative procedures (minitrial, summary jury trial, neutral evaluation) has promise. Choosing among these options will depend on such factors as the client's other goals and the extent to which each procedure is likely to overcome the barriers to settlement, factors that are discussed later in this article.

What if there were other employees with similar complaints of sexual harassment? In that case Stone might again want some formal declaration concerning the illegality of the conduct in question, which then could be used as a precedent in other cases. The company, viewing the problem from its vantage point, might have a similar preference for some type of reasoned adjudication (probably via a court decision, but possibly through arbitration or private judging).

But suppose instead that Stone is eager to keep her job and simply wants the annoying conduct to stop. Perhaps a transfer will accomplish that goal. If the company is willing to meet her halfway, it may be desirable to involve a mediator who can help facilitate this kind of solution in a quiet, confidential manner.

Of course, client goals may change as time passes, conditions change, and feelings wax or wane. Stone may start out bent on vengeance via public vindication and damages. But, as she considers giving up a job she finds satisfying, except for the harassment, her priority may shift from vindication and damages to retaining her job, if she can be assured that the employer has taken steps to protect her from harassment, and perhaps also to protect potential future victims.

These, then, are some of the considerations that lawyers and clients must examine with regard to processes that might meet client objectives. The value of various procedures in meeting specific client objectives is set forth in Table 1.

An important point to note is that the values assigned to each procedure in Table 1 (as well as in Table 2, which follows) are not based on empirical research but rather upon our own experience, combined with the views of other dispute resolution professionals. Moreover, the numerical values assigned to each procedure are not intended to be taken literally, but rather as a shorthand expression of the extent to which each procedure satisfies a particular objective.

If, for example, the client's goals are to maintain the relationship and receive a neutral opinion while also maximizing privacy, adding the numerical scores would lead to the following result: mediation 6; minitrial 8; summary jury trial 7; early neutral evaluation 6; arbitration 7; and court 3. One could not, however, conclude from these scores that the minitrial is the preferred procedure. Our analysis of the capacity of each procedure to meet various goals is not that precise. The most that one could conclude at this point in the analysis would be that some ADR procedure is preferable to court.

The next step in the analysis is to list the client's goals in order of priority. If the client is primarily interested in a prompt and inexpensive resolution of the dispute that also maintains or improves the parties' relationship—which is typical of *most* clients in *most*

Table 1
Extent to Which Dispute Resolution Procedures Satisfy Client Objectives

| | Procedures | | | | | |
| | Nonbinding | | | | Binding | |
Objectives	Mediation	Minitrial	Summary Jury Trial	Early Neutral Evaluation	Arbitration, Private Judging	Court
Minimize Costs	3	2	2	3	1	0
Speed	3	2	2	3	1	0
Privacy[a]	3	3	2	2	3	0
Maintain/ Improve Relationship[b]	3	2	2	1	1	0
Vindication[c]	0	1	1	1	2	3
Neutral Opinion[d]	0	3	3	3	3	3
Precedent[e]	0	0	0	0	2	3
Maximizing/ Minimizing Recovery	0	1	1	1	2	3

0 = Unlikely to satisfy objective	2 = Satisfies objective substantially
1 = Satisfies objective somewhat	3 = Satisfies objective very substantially

a. We believe that a summary jury trial and a neutral evaluation offer less privacy than the other ADR processes, in which the neutral is selected by the parties. In the summary jury trial, a judge or magistrate, as well as a jury, is present; in neutral evaluation, the neutral will typically be a court-appointed attorney. If, however, the neutral evaluator is selected by the parties, neutral evaluation will offer as much privacy as the other ADR processes. Conversely, if a mediator, minitrial neutral, or arbitrator were imposed by the court, that procedure would receive a lower privacy rating.

b. We have given early neutral evaluation a lower rating than the summary jury trial or the minitrial for the capacity to maintain relationships. While all three procedures are relatively brief and thus do little harm to the relationship, the summary jury trial and the minitrial typically involve negotiations between the principals, and such negotiations sometimes have the potential of mending a frayed relationship. If a particular early neutral evaluation were to involve negotiations between the principals, it would receive the same rating as the summary jury trial or the minitrial.

c. Since a need for vindication may be satisfied by an apology, mediation that results in an apology can satisfy the need for vindication. However, in our experience, apologies rarely occur in mediation [see pp. 137-139 of the casebook].

d. We have assigned the same ranking to all the procedures that provide any kind of neutral evaluation. But if one were to take account of the basis for making the evaluation, the procedures that provide for a full presentation of the evidence and arguments (namely, court and arbitration) would receive a higher score. A neutral evaluation which follows a full presentation of evidence and argument is likely to be given greater weight by the parties than is a neutral opinion based upon a more truncated presentation.

e. Although mediation normally seeks to provide a solution to the specific dispute, the parties could also agree on a new rule for future cases and thus obviate the need for a formal precedent.

business disputes—mediation is the preferred procedure. Mediation is the only procedure to receive maximum scores on each of these dimensions—cost, speed, and maintain or improve the relationship—as well as on assuring privacy, another interest which is present in many business disputes. It is only when the client's primary interests consist of establishing a precedent, being vindicated, or maximizing (or minimizing) recovery that procedures other than mediation are more likely to be satisfactory.

It should be clear from this discussion that our evaluation is based on assumptions concerning how ADR procedures are typically structured. If the procedures are structured differently, by court order or party design, the extent to which they will satisfy client goals will also differ. For example, mediation will generally cost the parties less and be faster than a summary jury trial or the minitrial, which require preparing to present evidence and arguments in a structured setting, but that is not always the case. Some parties will provide for a comparatively simple minitrial, with a minimum of preparation, while others will participate in a lengthy, somewhat formal mediation that will be expensive and time-consuming. Similarly, we have assumed that mediation is a process distinct from neutral evaluation, and have set the point values in Table 1 accordingly. But some mediators also perform evaluative functions, and some neutral evaluators attempt to mediate. Hence, Table 1 should be understood only as a general guide, subject to modification if the procedures involved differ from the norms on which the table was based.

A related point is that the processes listed in Tables 1 and 2 are discussed more or less in isolation. Often however, it is possible to blend or link different processes (e.g., mediation and evaluation) to develop a hybrid process. Indeed, Tables 1 and 2 can be used as a guide for designing a process that promises to achieve the client's objectives and, where settlement is sought, that is likely to overcome the envisioned impediments.

One final point concerning client goals: Some contend that ADR should be avoided altogether when one party will be sure to win if the matter is litigated. We disagree. First, the likely loser may be persuaded, through the use of one of the evaluative ADR procedures, to concede, thus sparing both parties the costs of litigation. An agreed-upon outcome is also more likely to be fully complied with than a court order. Alternatively, the likely loser may offer, in ADR, a settlement that is better in non-monetary terms than what could be achieved in litigation; such a settlement preserves, and often enhances, the parties' relationship. Thus, the prospect of a victory in litigation is not reason enough for avoiding ADR.

IMPEDIMENTS TO SETTLEMENT AND WAYS OF OVERCOMING THEM

In some circumstances, a settlement is not in the client's interest. For example, the client may want a binding precedent or may want to impress other potential litigants with its firmness and the consequent costs of asserting claims against it. Alternatively, the client may be in a situation in which there are no relational concerns; the only issue is whether it must pay out money; there is no pre-judgment interest; and the cost of contesting the claim is less than the interest earned on the money. In these and a small number of other situations, settlement will not be in the client's interest.

Still, a satisfactory settlement typically is in the client's interest. It is the inability to obtain such a settlement, in fact, that impels the client to seek the advice of counsel in the first place. The lawyer must consider not only what the client wants but also why the parties have been unable to settle their dispute, and then must find a dispute resolution procedure that is likely to overcome the impediments to settlement. Note, however, that, even though it may initially appear that the parties seek a settlement, sometimes an examination of the impediments to settlement reveals that at least one party wants something that settlement cannot provide (e.g., public vindication or a ruling that establishes an enforceable precedent).

The impediments to settlement, along with the likelihood that various ADR processes will overcome them, are set out in Table 2.

POOR COMMUNICATION

The relationship between the parties and/or their lawyers may be so poor that they cannot effectively communicate. Neither party believes the other, and each searches for hidden daggers in all proposals put forth by the other. An inability to communicate clearly and effectively, which impedes successful negotiations, is often, but not always, the result of a poor relationship. If, for example, the parties come from different cultural backgrounds, they may have great difficulty understanding and appreciating each other's concerns. Or, if there has been a long history of antagonism between the key players, all efforts to communicate are likely to be hampered by that antagonism.

Mediation is of great value in such situations. By controlling communications between the parties—keeping them physically apart, if necessary, and acting as a kind of translator—the mediator can literally "separate the people from the problem." (See Fisher, Ury and Patton, 1991). In addition, the mediator may encourage a discussion of the

Table 2
Likelihood that the ADR Procedure
Will Overcome Impediments to Settlement

Impediment	Mediation	Minitrial	Summary Jury Trial	Early Neutral Evaluation
		Procedures		
Poor Communication	3	1	1	1
Need to Express Emotions	3	1	1	1
Different View of Facts	2	2	2	2
Different View of Law	2	3	3	3
Important Principle	1	0	0	0
Constituent Pressure*	3	2	2	2
Linkage	2	1	1	1
Multiple Parties	2	1	1	1
Different Lawyer-Client Interests	2	1	1	1
Jackpot Syndrome	0	1	1	1

0 = Unlikely to overcome impediment
1 = Sometimes useful in overcoming impediment
2 = Often useful in overcoming impediment
3 = Most likely to be useful in overcoming impediment

*The values assigned to procedures other than mediation for their capacity to overcome the impediment of constituent pressure assume that the neutral does not have mediation authority. If the neutral does, those procedures should be assigned the same value as mediation.

factors leading to the dispute, and to the parties' inability to resolve the dispute on their own. How to improve the relationship, and thereby prevent future disputes, or at least to resolve them more easily, may also be considered.

To the extent that procedures such as the minitrial, the summary jury trial, and neutral evaluation permit the parties to address themselves to a neutral third party, rather than each other, these procedures are also somewhat useful in overcoming communications difficulties. However, unless the neutral in these processes plays both an evaluative and a mediatory role, which is typically not the case, these procedures are rated lower than mediation.

THE NEED TO EXPRESS EMOTIONS

At times, no settlement can be achieved until the parties have had the opportunity to express their views to each other about the dispute and each other's conduct. Such venting, combined with the feeling that one has been heard by the other party, has long been recognized as a necessary first step in resolving family and neighborhood disputes. Business disputes are no different. After all, they do not take place between disembodied corporations but between the people who manage those corporations, and who may have as much need to vent as anyone else involved in a dispute.

Mediation is clearly the preferred procedure when venting is necessary. By providing an informal atmosphere that encourages full participation by the disputants themselves, as well as by their lawyers, and by the presence of a neutral who can control the venting process, mediation can create a safe harbor for the parties to express their views fully. Some venting is possible in the evaluative ADR procedures; however, since their focus is on presenting evidence and argument concerning the rights of the parties, they are less hospitable to expressions of feelings.

DIFFERENT VIEWS OF FACTS

Did the defendant engage in the conduct that forms the basis of the plaintiff's complaint? Whose version of the facts is the finder of fact likely to believe? The greater the parties' disagreement on these matters, the more difficult settlement is likely to be.

Frequently, a skilled mediator can persuade the parties to put aside their factual dispute while at the same time agreeing on a mutually acceptable resolution of the dispute. If, however, the determination of disputed facts is essential to a resolution of the case, then some form of adjudication is required, such as a decision by a court, an arbitrator, or a private judge. A summary jury trial, neutral evaluation or minitrial, though not rendering a binding decision, may also aid in overcoming the impediment of conflicting evaluations of the facts by providing a neutral assessment of the case.

DIFFERENT VIEWS OF LEGAL OUTCOME IF SETTLEMENT IS NOT REACHED

Disputants often agree on the facts but disagree on their legal implications. The plaintiff asserts that, on the basis of the agreed-upon facts, he has a 90 percent likelihood of success in court; the defendant, with equal fervor, asserts that she has a 90 percent chance of success. While there may be a legitimate dispute over the likely outcome, both these estimates cannot be right.

Here, too, a mediator can often persuade the parties to resolve their dispute without determining which of their positions is "right." If not, a nonbinding appraisal of the likely outcome by an experienced neutral may be helpful in bringing about a settlement. An early neutral evaluation, a minitrial, or summary jury trial can provide such an appraisal.

ISSUES OF PRINCIPLE

If each of the disputing parties is deeply attached to some "fundamental" principle that must be abandoned or compromised in order to resolve the dispute, then resolution is likely to be difficult. Two examples: a suit challenging the right of neo-Nazis to march in a town where many Holocaust survivors live; and a suit by a religious group objecting to the withdrawal of life support systems from a comatose patient.

In view of the intensity of feelings in cases such as these, it is unlikely that evaluative techniques will be helpful in reaching a settlement. A mediator, however, may be able to find a creative way of reconciling (or bypassing) the seemingly conflicting values of the disputants by searching for a compromise that satisfies their differing interests. For example, in the neo-Nazi right-to-march dispute, the mediator might learn that the primary interest of the neo-Nazis is that of exercising their right to free speech, while the primary interest of the Holocaust survivors is not being confronted with disturbing reminders of the experiences they have suffered. Under these circumstances, mediation might lead to an agreement to allow the march, but to restrict its route to a part of town in which no Holocaust survivors live. To be sure, the parties might reach the same solution, on their own, but this is unlikely when emotions are high, the parties' relationship is terrible, and they must deal directly with each other, rather than through a mediator.

CONSTITUENCY PRESSURES

If one or more of the negotiators represents an institution or group, constituency pressures may impede agreement in two ways: different elements within the institution or group may have different interests in the dispute, or the negotiator may have staked her political or job future on attaining a certain result.

A mediator might deal with the first problem by mediating among the different parties that make up the organization, hoping to come up with a position that meets the divergent concerns. Such a technique is common in labor-management negotiations, where different groups of employees may have conflicting goals. Similarly, in an inter-corporate dispute, the production department of Corporation A may have one idea of what constitutes an acceptable settlement, the sales department may have another, and the finance department may have yet another. However united the corporation may appear to its opponent, a settlement proposal that affects different departments in a disparate fashion may reveal an underlying disunity that can be resolved only by mediation.

The mediator can solve the second problem—a negotiator's investment in a particular solution—by serving as a scapegoat, allowing the representative to blame the unsatisfactory outcome on the pressure exerted by the mediator. The other nonbinding processes can serve a similar function: the neutral's evaluation demonstrates to one or more of the constituent groups that its position is unlikely to prevail; hence, the settlement proposed by its representative is reasonable. A neutral who has the authority to evaluate and to mediate can use both techniques to deal with constituency pressures.

LINKAGE TO OTHER DISPUTES

The resolution of one dispute may have an effect on other disputes involving one or both parties. If so, this linkage will enter into their calculations, and may so complicate negotiations as to lead to an impasse. Here again, mediation holds much promise since the mediator can make explicit—and factor into the mediation—the linkage. Indeed, enlarging the agenda in many ways facilitates the mediation process.

For example, an automobile manufacturer in a dispute with one of its dealers concerning the dealer's right to sell autos made by other companies may ultimately be willing—for reasons specific to this dealer—to allow it to do so. But the manufacturer may so fear the effect of such an agreement on similar disputes with other dealers that the parties arrive at an impasse. It is possible that the manufacturer did not make this concern explicit in its negotiations with the dealer because it did not want the dealer to know it was engaged in similar disputes elsewhere. If the manufacturer confidentially discloses its concerns to the mediator, the mediator may be able to devise a settlement formula that meets the dealer's needs, yet preserves the manufacturer's position vis-à-vis other dealers. Alternatively, the mediator and the parties may devise an agreement that the manufacturer is willing to offer to all its dealers. The point is not that such a settlement could not have been reached without mediation but that the dynamic of mediation—in this case, the ability of the parties to make confidential disclosures to the mediator—can facilitate agreement.

This result might also be reached in the other nonbinding processes—the minitrial, the summary jury trial, and neutral evaluation—*if* the neutral in those processes plays a mediatory as well as an evaluative role, which is not always the case.

MULTIPLE PARTIES

When there are multiple parties, with diverse interests, the problems are similar to those raised by diverse constituencies and by issue linkages. Here, too, mediation will sometimes succeed in finding a balance of interests that satisfies all.

DIFFERENT LAWYER/CLIENT INTERESTS

Lawyers and clients often have divergent attitudes and interests concerning settlement. This may be a matter of personality (one may be a fighter, the other a problem solver) or of money. An attorney who is paid on an hourly basis stands to profit handsomely from a trial, and may be less interested in settlement than the client. On the other hand, an attorney paid on a contingent fee basis is interested in a prompt recovery without the expense of preparing for or conducting a trial, and may be more interested in settlement than is the client. It is in part because of this potential conflict of interest that most processes that seek to promote settlement provide for the client's direct involvement.

One way to remove the impediment created by different lawyer-client interests is to make explicit these differences. If a mediator conducts some meetings with clients separate from their lawyers, conflicting interests are likely to emerge. (Since both client and lawyer may, however, be concerned about such separate meetings, they are rarely conducted without the agreement of both.)

Suppose, instead, that the problem is not between lawyer and client on one side, but between opposing lawyers. Both clients are ready to settle the case on a reasonable basis, but the lawyers, for their own reasons, are intent on taking the case to trial. Such cases are often difficult to settle, and the best the mediator can do is to make sure that the costs—financial and otherwise—of the lawyers' kamikaze strategy are apparent to their clients. In fact, some mediators request attorneys to file premediation statements in which they estimate the cost and duration of a trial.

If the neutral plays a mediatory role and if the clients are present, the minitrial, the summary jury trial, and neutral evaluation can also be helpful in these situations.

THE "JACKPOT" SYNDROME

An enormous barrier to settlement often exists in those cases where the plaintiff is confident of obtaining in court a financial recovery far exceeding its damages, and the defendant thinks this is highly unlikely.

For example, the case may be one in which the controlling statute provides for the discretionary award of punitive damages to a successful plaintiff. If the underlying damage claim is for $10 million, and the plaintiff thinks that $50 million in punitive damages is a real possibility while the defendant does not, the vast disparity in case valuation may make settlement close to impossible. To be sure, one of the evaluative processes may affect one or the other party's estimate of the plaintiff's chance of hitting the jackpot, but the size of the jackpot may justify to the plaintiff the costs of litigation even if the odds against it are great. After all, millions of people play the lottery daily, even though their chances of success are infinitesimal; the temptation here is similar.

A RULE OF PRESUMPTIVE MEDIATION

Mediation will most often be the preferred procedure for overcoming the impediments to settlement. It has the greatest likelihood of overcoming all impediments except different views of facts and law, and the jackpot syndrome. Furthermore, a skilled mediator can often obtain a settlement without the necessity of resolving disputed questions of fact or law. Thus, there is much to be said for a rule of "presumptive mediation"—that mediation, if it is a procedure that satisfies the parties' goals, should, absent compelling indications to the contrary, be the first procedure used.

Under this approach, the mediator would first attempt to resolve the dispute by using customary mediation techniques. In doing so, the mediator would gain a clearer sense of the parties' goals and the obstacles to settlement than could be obtained by counsel prior to mediation. If mediation were not successful, the mediator could then make an informed recommendation for a different procedure. For example, if the parties were so far apart in their views of the facts or law that meaningful settlement negotiations could not take place, the mediator might recommend a referral to one of the evaluative procedures to move the parties closer to a common view of the facts and law. Once that had been accomplished, mediated settlement negotiations would recommence.

One of the strengths of this approach is that the mediator's process recommendation might be more readily accepted by both parties than would the suggestion of either of their attorneys, since attorney suggestions are sometimes suspected of being based on tactical considerations. Thus, the approach of "presumptive mediation" seems promising, particularly when the parties are having difficulty in agreeing upon an ADR procedure.

The presumption in favor of mediation would be overcome when the goals of one or both parties could not be satisfied in mediation, or mediation was clearly incapable of overcoming a major impediment to settlement. The most common situation in which this could occur would be when either party has a strong interest in receiving a neutral opinion, obtaining a precedent, or being vindicated, and is unwilling to consider any procedure that forecloses the possibility of accomplishing that objective.

THE PUBLIC PERSPECTIVE

For either a judge or a court employee responsible for recommending an ADR procedure, the question regarding barriers to settlement and how they can be overcome is the same as it is for individual disputants. The other question concerning goals is similar, but with a broader perspective. In lieu of asking what are the objectives one party wishes to achieve, as would counsel, the question is what both parties want to achieve. . . .

When a process selection is made from a public perspective, the public interest must also be considered. If the dispute is one in which a trial is likely to be lengthy, and so consume precious court time, there may be a public interest in referring the dispute to *some* form of ADR. Beyond that, one must ask if there is a public interest in having the dispute resolved pursuant to a *particular* procedure. For example, the referral of child custody disputes to mediation is required by law in several jurisdictions. The disputing parents may believe that they have no interest in a better relationship, but only in vindication, and hence prefer court to mediation. However, many states believe that a better relationship between the parents serves the public interest by improving the life of the child, and so mandate that child custody disputes go first to mediation.

The final question that must be asked in the public context is whether the public interest will be better served by a court decision than by a private settlement. If, for example, the dispute raises a significant question of statutory or constitutional interpretation, a court resolution might be preferable to a private settlement. While a court normally has no power to prevent parties from settling their own dispute, it does not follow that the court, as a public agency, should encourage or assist settlement in such a case.

Litigation may also serve the public interest better than mediation in cases of consumer fraud, which are often handled by the consumer protection division of an attorney general's office. Here not only the issue of *precedent,* but also the related issue of *recurring violations,* is key. The establishment of a general principle or a class remedy, by means of a class action, is clearly preferable to a series of repetitive and inconsistent mediations.

Another situation in which public adjudication is called for is when there is a *need for sanctioning.* If the defendant's conduct constitutes a public danger (assault with a deadly weapon, say, or maintaining a building in a grossly unsafe condition), ADR is inappropriate.

Finally, two more situations may militate against any use of ADR. First, *one or more of the parties may be incapable of negotiating effectively.* An unsophisticated pro se litigant, for example, may be vulnerable to exploitation in an ADR process. (On the other hand, such an individual, if not represented by a lawyer, may not fare better in court.) Second, court process may be required for some other reason: for example, *when serious issues of compliance or discovery are anticipated.*

[The authors then apply their analysis to three disputes, concluding as follows:]

CONCLUSION

In addressing the problem of "fitting the forum to the fuss," we have suggested two lines of inquiry: What are the disputants' goals in making a forum choice? And, if the disputants are amenable to settlement, what are the obstacles to settlement, and in what forum might they be overcome?

The fact that these inquiries rarely lead to a clear answer to the question of forum selection does not, we think, indicate that the analysis is faulty. Rather, it indicates that the question of forum selection ultimately turns on the extent to which the interests of the disputing parties (and sometimes of the public) will be met in various forums. Thus, the most that analysis can offer is a framework that clarifies the interests involved and promotes a thoughtful weighing and resolution of those interests.

Moreover such an inquiry concerning goals and impediments is often independently helpful in clarifying the dimensions of the basic dispute. When it then comes to exploring the ADR implications of that analysis, a sophisticated ADR user might well ask: "If these are my goals and my impediments, what kinds of third-party help do I need, and how can I design a procedure that provides that kind of help"? But we believe that the approach reflected in Tables 1 and 2 is more helpful for the typical ADR user.

As noted, the difficulties of process selection are substantially eased by a recognition that mediation, where it satisfies the client's goals, is typically the preferred procedure for overcoming the impediments to settlement. It is on this basis that we suggest a rule of presumptive mediation—that mediation, if it satisfies the client's goals, should, absent compelling indications to the contrary, be the first procedure used. If mediation is not successful, the mediator can then make an informed recommendation for a different procedure.

One final word: Although our focus here has been largely on disputes as they arise on their way to court or in court, the analysis is applicable in many other settings. For example, the parties to a long-term relationship, such as joint venturers, may request advice on appropriate processes for dealing with the disputes that may arise in their relationship. A similar request may come from a manufacturer routinely faced with claims by dissatisfied customers, or from a hospital faced with a spate of malpractice actions. In such situations, the focus will not be on an individual dispute but a series of actual or possible disputes. The attorney's task will be to analyze the client's interests in all those disputes, as well as the likely impediments to settlement, and to recommend a procedure or series of procedures that are likely to deal with those disputes efficiently and effectively.

Page 442.   After Question 11.9, add the following Note, article, text, and Question 11.10:

Note: Making the Decision to Settle — Litigation Risk Analysis

The purpose of most ADR procedures is to encourage settlement. But how do lawyers and clients know *when* to settle? What settlement offer is good enough to accept rather than proceed with litigation? Suppose that you have filed a complaint seeking $5 million in damages, and you receive a settlement offer of $1.5 million. Should you accept the offer or continue with the litigation? Presumably that depends on how you view the likelihood of success at litigation. That is where litigation risk analysis comes in.

G. SIEDEL, THE DECISION TREE: A METHOD TO FIGURE LITIGATION RISKS
B. Leader 18 (Jan.–Feb. 1986)

In recent years attorneys and clients have shown great interest in developing efficient, cost-effective methods for resolving disputes. Alternative dispute resolution has become popular inside and outside the court system. . . . Even when a dispute cannot be resolved by alternative methods, budgeting and financial planning have been used increasingly in the management of disputes.

A characteristic common to alternative dispute resolution and dispute management is the increased involvement by clients in legal decision-making. In turn, client involvement has created the need for improved attorney-client communication, especially with regard to questions that are difficult to analyze in complex litigation. Some of these are: What is the settlement value of the case? What is the chance for success? . . . The management technique of decision tree analysis can be used by clients and attorneys faced with these and related questions.

A BUSINESS DECISION

In 1983 the two professional basketball teams with the worst records, the Houston Rockets and the Indiana Pacers, qualified to participate in a coin flip to determine which team would have the rights to Ralph Sampson, the best college player available in the draft. A few days before the flip, Houston offered Indiana the following deal: If Indiana would agree not to participate in the coin flip—thus giving Houston the rights to Sampson—Houston would give Indiana a package that included a veteran player along with a combination of 1983 and 1984 Houston draft selections.

Suppose that Indiana Pacer management determined that the package was worth a net present value of $8 million, but that winning the flip—and Sampson—would net $16 million for the franchise. Losing the flip and acquiring the second pick, on the other hand, would net only $2 million. Should Indiana management accept the Houston offer?

A decision tree analysis of this problem begins with the development

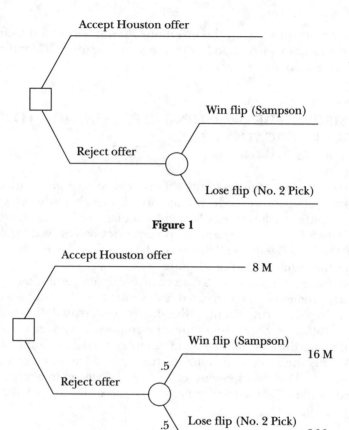

Figure 1

Figure 2

of a model called a decision tree, using a three-step process. First the problem is diagrammed in "tree" form, which allows the decision maker to visualize and distinguish events that can be controlled (decisions) from uncertain, uncontrollable events. Squares are used to represent decisions (decision nodes), while circles represent uncontrollable events (chance nodes). As Figure 1 shows, the decision faced by Indiana management is whether to accept or reject the Houston offer. These alternatives are represented on the tree by two "branches" drawn from the decision node. The coin flip, an uncontrollable event, is represented by the circle, from which are drawn "win" and "lose" branches. (See Figure 1.)

The second step involves assigning values to each endpoint on the tree. Values of $8 million (accept offer), $16 million (win flip) and $2 million (lose flip) have been assigned to the endpoints in Figure 2.

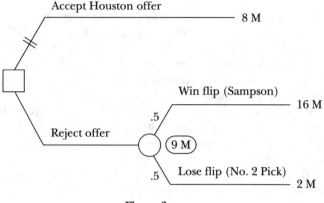

Figure 3

The third step is to assign probabilities for the uncontrollable events. In the Sampson case (assuming a fair coin), Indiana has a 50-50 chance of winning the flip. (See Figure 2.)

Once the model has been developed, the tree is "folded back," meaning a weighted average called the "expected value" is calculated for the chance nodes. The weighted average (expected value) of participating in the coin flip is $9 million (the sum of .5 × $16 million and .5 × $2 million). Using the decision tree to make the decision—that is, "playing the averages"—the Indiana management would choose to decline the Houston offer and participate in the coin flip. The decision is illustrated in Figure 3 by the two short vertical lines indicating that the "accept offer" branch has been severed. (See Figure 3.)

As a historical footnote, Indiana did participate in the flip and lost—thus having the second pick. Does this mean Indiana made the wrong decision? No, for if one accepts our factual assumptions, Indiana made a good decision from a weighted average standpoint. This illustrates a key feature of decision analysis—emphasis is placed on making good decisions, and a decision can be good even though the result is not favorable.

A LITIGATION EXAMPLE

The decision tree approach used in the Sampson case—building a model using the three-step approach and then using the model to make a decision—can be applied to litigation decisions. We will assume that you represent a software company that has sued a licensee, claiming that the licensee has infringed upon your client's copyright and violated the licensing agreement by producing its own version of the client's software. The defendant has made a settlement offer of $1.5 million, but you have determined that an injunction preventing the defendant from marketing its software would be worth $5 million to your client, after discounting cash flows and deducting $300,000 representing future legal expenses and the value of management time.

The key issues, and your evaluation of these issues, are as follows:

1. Is the defendant's software substantially similar to that of your client? (You conclude that you have a better than even chance of proving substantial similarity. . . .

2. Did the defendant have access to your client's software before developing its software? (You conclude that it is likely you will be able to prove access.)

3. Is your client's copyright valid? (You conclude that there is a high probability that the court will hold the copyright valid. . . .)

4. Even if the copyright is invalid, will your client prevail on a trade secrets theory? This raises two sub-issues. First, does federal copyright law pre-empt state trade secrets law? (You conclude that the probability is very high that there is no pre-emption.)

5. The second trade secrets issue is whether the defendant misappropriated your client's trade secrets. (You conclude that it is likely that you will prevail on this issue.)

Your client now raises a number of questions. Should the client accept the settlement offer of $1.5 million? What is the probability for success if you go to trial? . . .

In using decision tree analysis to answer these questions, the three-step process illustrated in the Sampson case is used to develop a model. First, the litigation is structured in decision tree form. Note in Figure 4 that there is one decision node and five chance nodes, representing the five key issues in the case. Second, endpoint values are assigned. Each "win" endpoint has been assigned a $5 million value, while the "lose" endpoints have a negative $300,000 value, representing future legal expenses and the value of management time. The $300,000 was deducted in calculating the $5 million "win" value. Also, a probability distribution—for example, a determination that there is a 50 percent chance of a $6 million return and a 50 percent chance that the return will be $4 million—has not been included in the analysis of values.

Finally, probabilities are assigned at each chance node. Each issue has been analyzed in probabilistic terms so at this stage we are essentially converting verbal statements into numbers. This conversion process often produces surprising results. For instance, the phrase "it is likely" used in discussing issues 2 and 5 might mean a 90 percent probability to the client, a 70 percent probability to you and a 40 percent probability to your partner. By converting verbal probabilities to numbers, you greatly enhance communication with clients and colleagues.

Once the model has been developed, you are ready to use the model to answer the questions raised in discussions with your client. For instance, should you settle the case or continue with the litigation? The process of "folding back" the tree by calculating the weighted averages—moving from right to left on the tree—reveals that the expected value of continuing with the litigation ($1.761 million) is greater than the settlement offer of $1.5 million. Consequently, if your client "played the averages," you would continue with the litigation. (See Figure 4 below.)

What is the probability for success if you go to trial? . . . [T]he decision tree shows two paths to success. The probability for success along each path is determined by multiplying the "win" probabilities for each issue along the path. Thus the chance for success on the copyright validity issue is .336 (.6 × .7 × .8) while the chance for success on the trade secrets theory is .05292 (.6 × .7 × .2 × .9 × .7). Combining the two figures, we arrive at an overall probability for success of 39 percent.

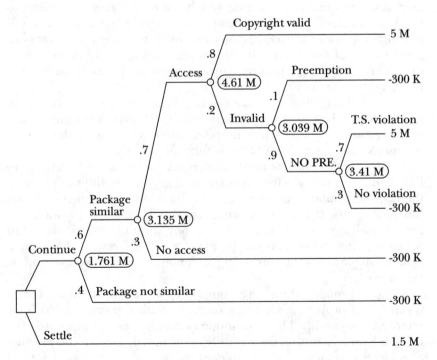

Figure 4

The decision tree model can be used in more sophisticated ways to answer other questions. . . . For instance, the model can be used in budgeting discovery costs, [or in] budgeting the costs for expert testimony that might change the chances for success, ... The model can also be used to take into account a client's attitude toward risk. A small start-up company, for example, might be less willing to play the averages than a larger, well-established company. To the small company, then, the "bird in the hand" offer of $1.5 million might be more attractive than "two in the bush"—the risky $5 million possibility. The client's attitude toward risk can be systematically factored into the decision tree analysis.

In addition to its value in making the decision of whether or not to accept a settlement offer, litigation risk analysis can also assist in reaching settlement. When dealing with disputing parties whose views of the litigation outcome are far apart, many mediators will ask each party to prepare a litigation risk analysis. In viewing the different analyses, the mediator can quickly determine which issue or issues are central to the disagreement. Sometimes simply uncovering the key issues and encouraging discussion focused on those issues is enough to bring about a settlement. If not, the mediator can suggest the use of an evaluative procedure to provide a neutral perspective on the key issues. This, too, may lead to settlement.

The use of litigation risk analysis as a settlement tool is not restricted to mediators. Just as a mediator can suggest that disputing parties use litigation risk analysis to pinpoint their differences, the parties themselves can agree to utilize this form of analysis.

There are two qualifications that must be noted with respect to litigation risk analysis. First, this type of analysis is of little value when the dispute primarily involves matters that cannot be converted into financial terms. It is difficult, for example, to imagine litigation risk analysis being of value in a child custody dispute (though Lax and Sebenius, 1986 (see casebook, p. 493, for full reference), have some creative suggestions for converting nonmonetary interests into monetary terms).

The other qualification pertaining to litigation risk analysis is that it is capable of projecting an image of mathematical precision that is far removed from reality. The "likelihood of success" percentages assigned to each issue are not mathematically determined, but are the product of subjective analysis. For example, in the hypothetical lawsuit set out in the article by Siedel, the plaintiff's probability of success on the copyright claim is stated to be .336 (or 33.6 percent). If, however, the probability of success on the three issues involved in the copyright claim were viewed as 50 percent, 60 percent, and 70 percent, instead of 60 percent, 70 percent, and 80 percent, the overall probability of success on the copyright claim would drop from 33.6 percent to 21 percent. And there is surely no way to be certain that the probability of success on any particular issue is 60 percent rather than 50 percent, or 80 percent rather than 70 percent.

One means of dealing with the subjectivity inherent in litigation risk analysis is to use a range of probabilities of success in lieu of the single probability point used by Professor Siedel. This was the approach used by the SEC representative on the Drexel Subclass B Executive Committee (Supplement, p. 75). In considering the probability of success on each issue relevant to a pending claim, the SEC representative determined whether there was absolutely no chance that the claimant would succeed (0 percent); that the chances ranged from slim to somewhat better than slim, but not 50-50 (10–30 percent); that the chances of success ranged from 50-50 to better than that, but surely not 100 percent (50–70 percent); or that the chances of success were virtually certain (90–100 percent). While this approach lacks the seeming precision of the approach used by Professor Siedel, it is perhaps a better representation of the combination of objective and subjective elements contained in litigation risk analysis.

Question

Question 11.10 You represent John Robinson, a 15-year-old boy who was employed in a restaurant operated by Barry's Burgers, Inc. Your client was badly burned when hot oil overflowed from a frier in which french fried potatoes were cooking.

You have brought suit against Barry's on two grounds. First, you allege that the fryer was improperly positioned, enabling the hot oil to overflow. Second, you allege that the fryer was loaded beyond capacity, causing the overflow. Damages have been stipulated to be $1 million, and you estimate expenses of trial and appeal at $100,000.

The practices that you challenge in this suit are standard operating procedure in all Barry's restaurants and have been the subject of five suits, all of which resulted in jury verdict. In two suits, Barry's prevailed on both the improper positioning issue and the overloading issue; in two suits, Barry's prevailed on the improper positioning issue, but lost on the overloading issue; in one suit, the plaintiff prevailed on both issues. All jury verdicts were upheld on appeal.

Barry's has made a settlement offer of $650,000. Should you recommend to your client that he accept that offer?

Page 449.   Add the following text and Question 11.11 before Exercise 11.1:

4.   Funding of ADR*

States and localities that are strapped for court funds typically look to one of two ways of funding alternatives. Some, like Washington, D.C., rely on a cadre of volunteers to fill this need. Many of these individuals are well-trained and highly qualified, and often bring a sense of enthusiasm and dedication not always matched by regular, paid employees.

Moreover, using a large number of volunteers—some of them influential citizens in the community—may be a good way of spreading the word about ADR. Some of these volunteers are lawyers who then use the techniques they have learned in their own cases.

There is, however, a more fundamental issue involved. If ADR is to develop responsibly as a practice, its practitioners need to be reasonably compensated.

This is true not only because Americans are all too prone to measure the value of services by how much we pay for them. There is also a more important point: What do we say to our talented young graduates who want to make a career of helping others resolve their disputes? That they should find some other work to support themselves and do dispute resolution in their spare time?

Sadly, the advice often given to young professionals who seek to enter the ADR market is "If you now have a paying job, don't quit it."

Of course, there may be sectors (such as neighborhood or community disputes) where the benefits of using volunteers are particularly salient. But if mediation is to be widely used in large-scale commercial and public policy disputes, then we cannot look solely to volunteers.

The other solution adopted in some jurisdictions (such as Florida and Texas) is to have the disputants pay the neutrals to whom the case has been referred.

From the point of view of most commercial clients, this may not pose much of a problem, provided some reasonable ceiling is set on the hourly rate charged by the neutrals, and some control is exercised by the court over the quality of the neutrals. For if a six-figure case can be satisfactorily and quickly resolved with the assistance of a skilled

*Adapted from Sander (1992).

104

third party who is paid a few hundred or even a few thousand dollars, that surely is a bargain for the litigants.

But that analysis, too, raises a more fundamental point. If the public justice system has an obligation to make available a range of dispute resolution options—as we believe it does—then the choice between various ADR options is unfairly biased if we make court adjudication available free or for a modest filing fee, but then charge the parties for alternative processes that may be more appropriate in a particular case.

Where the referral to ADR is mandatory there is the added question whether it is fair or legal to compel users of the public justice system to use certain alternative processes and then in effect to bill them for the cost.

Of course, as pointed out earlier, many of our court systems are in dire financial shape. Hence, it often may appear that the only realistic alternative to financing ADR through volunteers or party fees is to offer no ADR at all. That would be unfortunate. Moreover, even when public funds are more readily available, an additional problem may be the absence of sophisticated data showing the cost effectiveness of providing ADR options. So far most of the data have gone more to qualitative issues (see p. 155 of casebook). And adding free ADR options to the available court services almost always will increase the costs in the short run.

There is at least one other financing device that should be considered—add-on filing fees. In some jurisdictions, such as California, a surcharge has been added to the court filing fee, with these proceeds used to fund alternative processes.

If general public funds are not available, then this seems a fairer form of assessment, since the costs of improving the public dispute system are spread over all litigants, not simply imposed on the immediate disputants seeking to avail themselves of ADR procedures.

But all these measures should be seen as indirect, short-run solutions. In the long run, if we are to have a first-class public justice system, available freely to all, then we must find the necessary public funds to pay for it.

Question

11.11 The preceding essay takes the view that ADR will not develop responsibly if practitioners are not reasonably compensated. In some communities, however, mediators receiving court referrals are nearly all volunteers, even in the federal courts situated within those communities. Volunteer mediators include senior partners of major firms and others who are willing to undergo mediation training and to donate their time for about eight cases per year. In these communities, some speculate that if the court paid mediators, those previously drawn to mediate because of public spirit would withdraw, leaving mediators who would be attracted by the relatively low public fees. In this alternate view, a switch to compensated mediators for the average case would result in higher costs for the courts and in worse rather than better mediators.

Given the doubts about how ADR will develop, would you encourage a court planning a mediation program to aim for compensated or volunteer mediators?

Page 450.   Add the following to the References:

BODILY, Samuel (1991) "When Should You Go to Court," *Harv. Bus. Rev.* 103 (May/June).

CPR INSTITUTE FOR DISPUTE RESOLUTION (1994) "Dispute Resolution Clauses: A Guide for Drafters of Business Agreements," 12 *Alternatives* 66.

SANDER, Frank E.A. (1992) "Paying for ADR," *A.B.A. J.* 105 (Feb.).

SANDER, Frank E.A., and Stephen B. GOLDBERG (1994) "Fitting the Forum to the Fuss: A User-Friendly Guide to Selecting an ADR Procedure," 10 *Neg. J.* 49.

SIEDEL, George J. (1986) "The Decision Tree: A Method to Figure Litigation Risks," *B. Leader* 18 (Jan.–Feb.).

Chapter 12

Dispute Resolution Exercises

Page 465.   After Exercise 12.11, add Exercises 12.12, 12.13, 12.14, and 12.15:

EXERCISE 12.12: SATCOM, INC. V. TELECOM

Worldsat, a joint venture company, was established to seek a license for, and, if successful, to operate, a worldwide satellite communications system intended to increase the range and the reliability of portable cellular phones. One of the two joint venturers, Satcom, Inc., had primary responsibility for satellite construction; the other, Telecom, which was composed of three corporations acting as equal partners, had primary responsibility for satellite operations.

Both joint venturers knew that they would have to invest substantial amounts of money in this project and that there was no guarantee that they would receive a license. (The Federal Communications Commission [FCC] had announced that only one applicant would be granted a license.) The bulk of the up-front investment was to consist of designing and building a prototype satellite. After lengthy negotiations with Telecom's general counsel, Satcom's president agreed to undertake that task, at Satcom's expense, on the condition that if the license were awarded to another applicant, Satcom would be reimbursed for 50 percent of its expenses, plus interest, by Telecom. The contract also contained a *force majeure* clause, which provided that if the joint venture could not be carried out for reasons beyond the control of either party, neither party would be liable to the other.

After Satcom had completed its work, at a cost of $400 million, the FCC announced that, because of limited world spectrum availability, it would not grant a license to any of the applicants. Satcom demanded

107

$200 million, plus interest, from Telecom on the basis of the reimbursement clause. Telecom refused, arguing that the reimbursement clause applied only if a license were granted to another applicant, not if *no* license were granted. The latter situation, Telecom argued, was controlled by the *force majeure* clause, under which no recovery was available. Satcom responded that Telecom ignored the purpose of the cost allocation provision, which was to share the loss if the joint venture failed because it did not receive a license. This provision, designed specifically for this contingency, argued Satcom, ought to prevail over the general *force majeure* clause.

Satcom brought suit against Telecom seeking $200 million in damages. After three years of discovery and motions, nothing has been resolved. Each party has incurred approximately $2 million in attorney's fees and expenses to date, and each anticipates spending at least another $2 million in fees and expenses if the case goes to trial. Demands on executives' time have been and will continue to be great.

Settlement negotiations, carried on by Satcom's and Telecom's general counsel, have been desultory and marked by frequent accusations of bad faith. Telecom's general counsel insists that he negotiated only a limited reimbursement provision with Satcom and has let it be known that he regards Satcom's contention to the contrary as frivolous and motivated by the desire of Satcom's president to keep his job. Telecom's most recent settlement offer, which it characterizes as a "nuisance payment," was $4 million; Satcom's most recent demand was $160 million. No trial date has yet been set, and the judge estimates that it will be at least two years to trial.

If you were Satcom's outside counsel, what advice might you give Satcom regarding an appropriate dispute resolution procedure?

EXERCISE 12.13: A NEIGHBORHOOD DISPUTE

Smith and Jones are neighbors who share a driveway. In the past year, there have been numerous instances in which one of them has blocked the other's car, leading to angry exchanges and threats of physical harm. Last week, things finally reached a boiling point. When Smith once again blocked Jones's car, Jones came out of his house and socked Smith on the jaw. Smith called the local police and said he wanted to file an assault charge against Jones.

If you were the prosecutor, would you refer this case to the Neighborhood Justice Center for mediation?

EXERCISE 12.14: THOMAS V. EAGLE RIFLE CO.

You represent the parents of Roger Thomas, a 15-year-old boy who accidentally shot and killed himself while playing with an air rifle manufactured by Eagle Rifle Co. Shortly after Roger's death, his parents brought suit against Eagle for negligence in manufacturing the rifle involved, as well as for breach of warranty in manufacturing a product not reasonably safe for purchasers in the age-group for which the product was intended. The suit seeks $5 million in damages.

According to Mr. and Mrs. Thomas, they intend to use whatever amount they recover from Eagle to warn other parents about the dangers of air rifles. If they receive any amount close to the $5 million they have demanded, they plan to establish a charitable foundation to carry out this publicity campaign. They do not, however, want this case to go to trial, as reliving the events leading to their son's death would be extremely painful for them.

You are aware of three similar suits against Eagle which have gone to trial in the last two years. In each of those suits, Eagle received a jury verdict in its favor. In two other suits, Eagle prevailed on motions for summary judgment. In each case its defense has been the same: Eagle takes all precautions to manufacture air rifles that are as safe as possible. Additionally, Eagle has spent substantial sums to publicize the inherent risks associated with air rifles. Under these circumstances, neither negligence nor breach of warranty claims are well-founded. Additionally, Eagle typically asserts that the purchaser has assumed whatever risks are inherent in the use of its air rifles.

What dispute resolution procedure would best serve your clients' interests in this matter? How would you estimate your chances of reaching agreement with counsel for Eagle on a dispute resolution procedure?

EXERCISE 12.15: CAROLINE'S DONUT SHOP*

Pleasantown is a comfortably affluent suburb of wide, tree-lined streets and graceful gardens. It sits on the outskirts of Metropolis, one of the major cities of the state. During the past two years, and particularly in the last several months, Metropolis has become home to a growing number of refugees from the nation of Libertad, where civil war has

*This exercise was written by Cheryl B. McDonald, Pepperdine University School of Law, and Nancy Rogers and is reprinted with their permission.

threatened lives and has led to a breakdown in the market system for their crops and products.

The city planners of Pleasantown placed the town's "main drag" of charming shops, trees, and restaurants on High Street, a road leading directly into Metropolis. A bus regularly travels between the two communities, taking city workers into town and bringing back shoppers. Caroline's Donut Shop is located on High Street near a bus stop. Like most of Pleasantown's shops, Caroline's provides parking for only one or two cars; most of Caroline's business comes from people waiting for the bus or enjoying a shopping stroll.

Over the past few months large numbers of Libertadan men have been hanging around Caroline's Donut Shop. They arrive early in the morning and usually lean against the walls outside Caroline's and neighboring businesses, drinking coffee, talking to one another, and waiting.

Every weekday morning, just as the commuter traffic begins to build, gardeners and construction contractors, among others, come cruising slowly along High Street searching for day workers from among the gathered Libertadans. Because there is no place to park, workers rush out to cars and trucks in the street in order to guarantee their selection for one job or another. Some of the potential employers have hired particular men in the past, and they wait with their motors running until others have cleared a path for their favorites to get close enough to jump into the truck. The frenzy is usually over in an hour or two—most contractors get an early start. But with lowered demands in recent weeks, more and more of the Libertadans are left on the sidewalk.

Most of the workers have bus fare for only one round trip per day. Many are illiterate or speak only Spanish. Some are in the country illegally. As a result, they have little prospect for other work; they stay at Caroline's just in case someone has a late job. Some drink coffee or soda, leaving the empty containers on the curb or sidewalk. Some step out into the street to wave at passing vehicles. One or two follow women with their eyes as they pass by, sometimes making comments or laughing behind their backs. Some have used nearby lawns and bushes as toilets.

The homeowners and merchants of Pleasantown have become more and more upset over the last few months by the men gathering in front of Caroline's. The merchants feel that having the men hanging around makes potential customers (most of whom are women in the middle of the day) uneasy and that their businesses are suffering as a result. They have expressed concern that someone will be killed as people run out and have conversations in the street. The residents also complain about the disruption of early morning traffic. They have requested increased police patrols around the area, but that does not seem to have helped.

110

Last month some of the unhappy residents of Pleasantown put pressure on the Town Council to pass an ordinance prohibiting any person from standing on the street or highway to solicit employment from anyone in a motor vehicle and prohibiting any occupant of a stopped or parked motor vehicle from hiring a person from the vehicle. Although the owner of Caroline's tried to argue that the Libertadans were not hurting anyone (in fact, their labor was making Pleasantown an *affordable*, beautiful place to live) and were nice people, the ordinance passed unanimously.

As soon as the Libertadans found out about the ordinance, they realized what a threat it was to their ability to make a living. The gathering place at Pleasantown is conveniently accessible by cheap transportation and offers the only steady work to be found. The men feel that what little bread they can feed their families is being snatched from their mouths. Even though they have no money, they must fight back. They have enlisted the support of a group in the local parish. One of the church members, who is fluent in Spanish, has been asked to be their spokesperson and to accompany them as they come to you for help.

You are aware that a case involving a similar situation was filed in another jurisdiction. The complaint raised First and Fourteenth Amendment issues. Unfortunately, the court in that case refused to enjoin enforcement of the ordinance.

You will be assigned to a small group. Working together, prepare one member to advise your clients, the Libertad day workers, on the following questions:

1. Assume that no action has been taken since the passage of the ordinance. What are the advantages or disadvantages for the clients of trying mediation in this case?

2. If a mediation will be arranged for this case, what is the best timing in relation to litigation (i.e., filing the action, conducting formal or informal discovery, filing motions, etc.)?

3. Assume for questions 3 through 6 that the parties have agreed in principle to mediate the case. Who should attend? Parties only? Lawyers only? Both? Who should participate?

4. If representatives of the laborers, the merchants, the homeowners, and the Town Council will attend the mediation, should there be ground rules about disclosures to others, including the press? What ground rules do you propose?

5. How should the mediator(s) be selected? What qualifications should the mediator(s) have?

6. If the clients will attend the mediation session, how will you prepare them for the mediation session? How do you anticipate that your role as counsel in the mediation will differ from your role representing the clients at trial?

Collected References

BERCOVITCH, Jacob, and Jeffrey RUBIN (1992) *Mediation in International Practice*. New York: St. Martin's.

BERNSTEIN, Lisa (1993) "Understanding the Limits of Court-Connected ADR: A Critique of Federal Court-Annexed ADR Programs," 141 *U. Pa. L. Rev.* 2169.

BODILY, Samuel (1991) "When Should You Go to Court," *Harv. Bus. Rev.* 103 (May/June).

BRETT, Jeanne M., Stephen B. GOLDBERG, and William L. URY (1994) "Managing Conflict: The Strategy of Dispute Systems Design," 6 Bus. Wk. Executive Briefing Service.

BRYAN, Penelope E. (1992) "Killing Us Softly: Divorce Mediation and the Politics of Power," 40 *Buff. L. Rev.* 441.

BRYAN, Penelope E. (1994) "Reclaiming Professionalism: The Lawyer's Role in Divorce Mediation," 28 *Fam. L.Q.* 177.

BUSH, Robert A. Baruch (1992) *The Dilemmas of Mediation Practice*. Washington, D.C.: National Institute for Dispute Resolution.

BUSH, Robert A. Baruch, and Joseph P. FOLGER (1994) *The Promise of Mediation*. San Francisco: Jossey-Bass.

BUSH, Robert A. Baruch (1994) "Symposium: Dilemmas of Mediation Practice," *J. Disp. Resol.* 1.

CENTER FOR DISPUTE SETTLEMENT (1992) *National Standards for Court-Connected Mediation Programs*. Washington, D.C.: CDS.

COMMISSION ON THE FUTURE OF WORKER-MANAGEMENT RELATIONS (1994) *Report and Recommendations*. Washington, D.C.: Government Printing Office.

CONDLIN, Robert J. (1992) "Bargaining in the Dark: The Normative Incoherence of Lawyer Dispute Bargaining Role," 51 *Md. L. Rev.* 1.

CPR INSTITUTE FOR DISPUTE RESOLUTION (1994) "Dispute Resolution Clauses: A Guide for Drafters of Business Agreements," 12 *Alternatives* 66.

DAUER, Edward A. (1994) *Manual of Dispute Resolution*. Colorado Springs: Shepards-McGraw Hill.

DISPUTE RESOLUTION MAGAZINE (1994) "Face Off: Should Binding Arbitration Clauses Be Prohibited in Consumer Contracts?" (Summer), p. 4.

FAURE, Guy, and Jeffrey RUBIN (1993) *Culture and Negotiation*. Newbury Park, Cal.: Sage.

FISCHER, Karla, Neil VIDMAR, and Rene ELLIS (1993) "The Culture of Battering and the Role of Mediation in Domestic Violence Cases," 46 *SMU L. Rev.* 2117.

FRIEDMAN, Gary (1993) *A Guide to Divorce Mediation*. New York: Workman.

GAGNON, Andre G. (1992) "Ending Mandatory Divorce Mediation for Battered Women," 15 *Harv. Women's L.J.* 272.

GALANTER, Marc, and Mia CAHILL (1994) " 'Most Cases Settle': Judicial Promotion and Regulation of Settlements," 46 *Stan. L. Rev.* 1339.

GIBSON, Kevin V. (1992) "Confidentiality in Mediation: A Moral Reassessment," *J. Disp. Resol.* 25.

GOLDBERG, Stephen B. (1994) "Reflections on Negotiated Rulemaking," 9 Wash. Law. 42 (Sept./Oct.).

GORMAN, Robert A. (forthcoming) "The Gilmer Decision and the Private Arbitration of Public Law Disputes," *U. Ill. L. Rev.* (June 1995).

HAYNES, John M. (1994) *The Fundamentals of Family Mediation.* Albany: State University of New York.

HERMANN, Michele (1994) "New Mexico Research Examines Impact of Gender and Ethnicity in Mediation," *Disp. Resol. Mag.* 10 (Fall).

HERMANN, Michele, Gary LAFREE, Christine RACK, and Mary Beth WEST (1993) *The Metrocourt Project Final Report.* Albuquerque: University of New Mexico Center for the Study and Resolution of Disputes.

KATZ, Lucy (1993) "Compulsory Alternative Dispute Resolution and Volunteerism: Two-Headed Monster or Two Sides of the Coin?" *J. Disp. Resol.* 1.

KEILITZ, Susan (1993) *National Symposium on Court-Connected Dispute Resolution Research.* Williamsburg: National Center for State Courts.

KOLB, Deborah M., and Associates (1994) *When Talk Works: Profiles of Mediators.* San Francisco: Jossey-Bass.

KOVACH, Kimberlee (1994) *Mediation: Principles and Practice.* St. Paul: West.

LEWIS, Michael (forthcoming) "Advocacy in Mediation: One Mediator's View," *Disp. Resol. Mag.* (Fall 1995).

MCEWEN, Craig A., and Nancy H. ROGERS (1994) "Bring the Lawyers into Divorce Mediation," *Disp. Resol. Mag.* 8–10 (Summer).

MCEWEN, Craig A., Richard MAIMAN, and Lynn MATHER (1994) "Lawyers, Mediation, and the Management of Divorce Practice," 28 *L. & Soc'y Rev.* 249.

MCEWEN, Craig A., Nancy H. ROGERS, and Richard J. MAIMAN (1995) "Bring in the Lawyers: Challenging the Dominant Approaches to Ensuring Fairness in Divorce Mediation," 79 *Minn. L. Rev.* 601.

MACNEIL, Ian (1992) *American Arbitration Law.* Boston: Little, Brown.

MACNEIL, Ian, Richard SPEIDEL, and Thomas STIPANOWICH (1994) *Federal Arbitration Law: Agreements, Awards, and Remedies Under the Federal Arbitration Act.* Boston: Little, Brown.

METZLOFF, Thomas (1992) "Reconfiguring the Summary Jury Trial," 41 *Duke L. J.* 806.

MNOOKIN, Robert H. (1993) "Why Negotiations Fail: An Exploration of Barriers to the Resolution of Conflict," 8 *Ohio St. J. on Disp. Resol.* 235.

MNOOKIN, Robert H., and Ronald J. GILSON (1994) "Disputing Through Agents: Cooperation and Conflict Between Lawyers in Litigation," 94 *Colum. L. Rev.* 509.

MNOOKIN, Robert H., and Ronald J. GILSON (1994) "Cooperation and Conflict Between Litigators," 12 *Alternatives* 125.

NEGOTIATION JOURNAL (1993) "Who Really Is a Mediator? A Special Section on the Interim Guidelines," Vol. 9, p. 290.

Collected References

NELLE, Andreas (1992) "Making Mediation Mandatory: A Proposed Framework," 7 *Ohio St. J. on Disp. Resol.* 287.

PLAPINGER, Elizabeth, and Margaret SHAW (1992) *Court ADR: Elements for Program Design.* New York: Center for Public Resources Institute for Dispute Resolution.

PORTLAND MEDIATION SERVICE (1992) *Mediation in Cases of Domestic Abuse: Helpful Option or Unacceptable Risks? The Final Report of the Domestic Abuse and Mediation Project.* Portland, ME: Portland Mediation Service.

PRINCEN, Thomas (1992) *Intermediaries in International Conflict.* Princeton: Princeton University Press.

RESNIK, Judith (1994) "Whose Judgment? Vacating Judgments, References for Settlement, and the Role of Adjudication at the Close of the Twentieth Century," 41 *U.C.L.A. L. Rev.* 1471.

RISKIN, Leonard (1993) "Mediator Orientations, Strategies and Techniques," *Alternatives* 111 (Sept.).

ROGERS, Nancy H., and Craig A. MCEWEN (1994) *Mediation: Law, Policy, Practice,* 2d ed. New York: Clark Boardman Callaghan.

ROLPH, Elizabeth, Erik MOLLER, and Laura PETERSON (1994) *Escaping the Courthouse: Private Alternative Dispute Resolution in Los Angeles.* Santa Monica: Rand Institute for Civil Justice.

ROSENBERG, Joshua (1991) "In Defense of Mediation," 33 *Ariz. L. Rev.* 467.

ROSENBERG, Joshua D., and H. Jay FOLBERG (1994) "Alternative Dispute Resolution: An Empirical Analysis," 46 *Stan. L. Rev.* 1487.

RUBIN, Jeffrey, and Jeswald SALACUSE (1993) "International Negotiation," *Alternatives* 95 (July).

SANDER, Frank E.A. (1992) "Paying for ADR," *A.B.A. J.* 105 (Feb.).

SANDER, Frank E.A., and Stephen B. GOLDBERG (1994) "Fitting the Forum to the Fuss: A User-Friendly Guide to Selecting an ADR Procedure," 10 *Neg. J.* 49.

SANDER, Frank E.A., and Christopher M. THORNE (forthcoming 1995) "Dispute Resolution in the Construction Industry: The Role of Dispute Review Boards,"— *Construction L. Rep.* 2d —.

SHELL, G. Richard (1991) "When Is It Legal to Lie in Negotiations?" *Sloan Mgmt. Rev.* 93 (Spring).

SHERMAN, Edward (1993) "Court-Mandated Alternative Dispute Resolution: What Form of Participation Should be Required?" 46 *SMU L. Rev.* 2079.

SIEDEL, George J. (1986) "The Decision Tree: A Method to Figure Litigation Risks," *B. Leader* 18 (Jan.–Feb.).

SINGER, Linda R. (1994) *Settling Disputes: Conflict Resolution in Business, Families, and the Legal System,* 2d ed. Boulder: Westview.

SLAIKEU, Karl, and Ralph HASSON (1992) "Not Necessarily Mediation: The Use of Convening Clauses in Dispute Systems Design," 8 *Neg. J.* 331.

SOCIETY OF PROFESSIONALS IN DISPUTE RESOLUTION (1994) *Ensuring Competence and Quality in Dispute Resolution* (draft report of the Commission on Qualifications).

TREUTHART, Mary Pat (1993) "In Harm's Way? Family Mediation and the Role of the Attorney Advocate," 32 *Golden Gate U.L. Rev.* 717.